IN PRAISE OF . . .

Christian Answers Course is everything you wanted to know about Christianity wrapped up in one book!

— DRAKE MARIANI, FOUNDER, MEMLOK BIBLE
MEMORY SYSTEM

A treasure trove of thoughtful responses to the most commonly asked questions about the Christian faith.

— PHIL FULLER, SENIOR PASTOR, RANCHO
MURIETA COMMUNITY CHURCH

May the *Christian Answers Course* find its way into the hands of many spiritual seekers, newborn Christians, and disciple-making defenders of the faith...

— BOB LAWLER, MISSION CATALYST, REDWOOD
EMPIRE BAPTIST ASSOCIATION

...a great insightful resource for anyone seeking clear, biblical answers to some of life's most pressing spiritual questions. Who isn't looking for that?

— EARL ESTEP, MEN'S PASTOR, CREEKSIDE
CHRISTIAN CHURCH

...a practical and biblical guide ... has the potential to influence non-believers and believers alike.

— BUCK ROGERS, PASTOR OF DISCIPLESHIP, GRACE CHURCH, WACO

A new Christian classic! ... a great resource for Christians and seekers of truth.

— NORM PATRICIA PURVIS, WYCLIFFE BIBLE TRANSLATORS

If you have a friend who is honestly seeking answers regarding faith, *Christian Answers Course* is a great choice.

— MIKE RILEY, FORMER SENIOR PASTOR, OPEN DOOR CHURCH

... this comprehensive and compelling book provides thoughtful and clear reasons for faith.

— MIKE SLONE, STAFF REPRESENTATIVE, THE NAVIGATORS

Wonderful resource. Well researched and lays a solid foundation... Highly recommended.

— PATRICK PARKS, LEAD PASTOR, BODEGA BAY CHURCH

CHRISTIAN ANSWERS COURSE

CLEAR ANSWERS TO CRUCIAL FAITH QUESTIONS

CHRISTOPHER R. LOSEY

Publish Authority

ISBN 978-1-954000-93-3 (Paperback)
ISBN 978-1-954000-94-0 (eBook)

All Scripture quotes taken from the New American Standard Bible (NASB) and are written in italics—underlinings added by the author, for emphasis, Copyright 1960, 1962, 1963, 1968, 1971, 1972, 1973, 1975, 1977, 1995 by the Lockman Foundation

Published 2025 by Publish Authority,
300 Colonial Center Parkway, Suite 100
Roswell, GA USA
PublishAuthority.com

Printed in the United States of America

Dedicated to my wife, Sharon, who is my best friend and has been a constant source of encouragement to me for the past fifty years we have been married!

CONTENTS

But sanctify Christ as Lord in your hearts, always being ready to make a defense to everyone who asks you to give an account for the hope that is in you, yet with gentleness and reverence.

—1 PETER 3:15 (NASB)

FOREWORD

Over the nearly 40 years that I have known Chris Losey he has been a friend, a missionary supporter, a pastor and eventually a Board member of the ministry of which I was president. His passion for sharing the Truth that explains a Biblical, Christian and Theological understanding of human existence that resides in Holy Scripture has been unwavering.

In his book *Christian Answers Course*, Losey's heart of a Pastor is combined with clear apologetics that affirm the sheep that know the voice of the True Shepherd, Jesus, and enlightens the sheep that have not found the pasture yet. Both flocks would benefit from this book that is built for authentic Christian understanding and sharing.

Eight Big "Life Question" chapters like *Does God Exist?* or *Is Evolution True?* invite the reader to explore succinct ways to unpack the question and build a base of knowledge on how followers of Jesus might answer those questions. Each chapter will enlighten and inspire and inform both the Christian and the seeker to a better understanding of the lengths the True Shepherd went to in revealing His Truth.

Dr. Timothy Conrad
Founder and President Emeritus, UW Sports Ministry

PREFACE

Initially, my purpose in answering the questions now addressed in this book was to solidify my own faith. As I researched and answered the questions, I felt my own faith grow. I also discovered that many people were seeking answers to the same and other questions for themselves. That is when I realized that a book like Christian Answers Course had the potential to influence both non-believers and believers, alike. Non-believers could see how placing their faith in Christ is not a blind leap of faith, but instead a reasonable step of faith. Believers, on the other hand could have their faith strengthened and at the same time be learning things they could share with family and friends who showed an interest in the things of God. I also saw the potential of it being used in quarterly Sunday School Classes, Bible studies, and one-on-one or small group discipleship. It is my hope that as you read this book it will help you either find Christ, be strengthened in your faith, or give you a good tool you can use to help others grow in their relationship with God. Happy reading!

INTRODUCTION

Today, many people have legitimate questions about God and religion. If you are honestly looking for answers related to God and religion, "The Answers Course" is for you. It has been designed to give solid answers to many important questions.

As you go through the course, hopefully, many of your questions will be answered, and you will see why believing in God is not a blind leap of faith but a reasonable step of faith.

As you read, you will notice a degree of repetition. Many times, a topic is introduced in one section, with explanation and illustration. Later, when that same topic recurs for further discussion, I have deliberately included that same material again, for the reader's convenience, to eliminate the need for leafing back to find it in its original location.

I believe God gave us our minds so we can think and learn. Part of the learning process is asking questions and seeking answers. In this regard, I hope this material is helpful to you. If you have further interest in any of the topics in this book, additional resources are presented in the appendix.

CHAPTER
ONE
DOES GOD EXIST?

When it comes to spiritual things, there is no more basic question than, "Does God exist?" Those who believe in God sometimes do so for no other reason than, "That is what I was taught in church." Likewise, those who don't believe sometimes have less-than-solid reasons.

Which of the following reasons for believing or not believing in God's existence do you think are reasonable?

- I believe God exists because that's what my parents told me.
- I don't believe there is a God because I can't see Him.
- I believe there is a God because it seems the right thing to do.
- I don't believe because there is too much evil in the world.

None of these reasons is built on strong evidence. They are simply based on what others have said or on personal opinions. If a person believes there is a God, he should have a better reason than, "That is what I was taught in church." Likewise, if a person rejects God's existence, it should be based on something more than not having seen God.

Is the question, "Does God exist?" a fair one? Some people say "yes," others "no." The nay-sayers might argue, "A person should not need reasons to believe God exists because faith is central to religion. After all, the Bible teaches, *And without faith it is impossible to please Him, for he who comes to God must believe that He is, and that He is a rewarder of those who seek Him* (Hebrews 11:6)."

There is no doubt that faith is important when it comes to religion but consider for a moment two kinds of faith: one is blind faith, the other reasonable faith. Blind faith is a leap in the dark. It believes in God without good evidence. Reasonable faith believes in God based on solid evidence. If there is a God, it seems reasonable that He would give people sufficient evidence so they could have reasonable faith. To leave them in the dark would seem out of character, especially if God is loving, as some people claim.

This brings up the question, "Is there evidence for God's existence?" The answer is a resounding "Yes."

Before examining the evidence, it is also important to state that God's existence cannot be proven scientifically. God cannot be put in a test tube and measured, but neither can anger, loneliness, joy, sorrow, or love; yet we all know these things exist.

Beyond the test tube, there is other strong evidence for God's existence. A person might be able to explain away some of the evidence, but when taken in total and considered objectively, it is overwhelming. Faith is still involved, but it is not blind faith; it is quite reasonable.

When talking with a scientist, one atheist said, "I know for certain there is no God."

"How do you know?" asked the scientist.

"I just know," said the atheist.

The scientist then politely replied, "Friend, consider this. It has been said that of all there is to know, scientists postulate that all men who have ever lived only know one-tenth of one percent. Put another way, if all the knowledge in the universe was contained in a thousand-page book, all men together would understand the content of one page. Any one man might know one word on that page. For you to say emphatically, 'There is no God,' is like a person opening a thousand-page book at random, reading one word, closing the book, and then saying dogmatically, 'The author has no grasp of his subject.' If you say you are an agnostic and aren't sure about God's existence, that would be understandable. But to say confidently, 'There is no God,' is an unsupportable position indeed."

I am personally convinced that people reject God's existence not because of the evidence but because they choose to.

EVIDENCE FOR THE EXISTENCE OF GOD

1. Consciousness of God

The first evidence for God's existence is man's consciousness of God. This may sound insignificant, but it is interesting that humans everywhere have what might be called a "God-consciousness." Put another way, it is accurate to say people are incurably religious. No matter where a person goes in the world, people worship something: the sun, an idol, trees, animals, or some other god. As far as we know, humans are the only creatures with this consciousness.

The question arises, "Where did this consciousness of God come from?" I believe the only reasonable answer is it came from God! It seems God created a spiritual void in all humans that can only be filled by Him. People know instinctively that God exists and, in general, long to reach out to Him. The fact that some people reject God is proof they possess a God-consciousness.

If people are honest with themselves, some would admit their rejection of God simply comes out of a desire to run their own lives. They do not want to submit themselves to anyone, especially God. To do so would mean they might have to change the way they live. I know this is true because I was one of these people.

2. Cause and Effect

A second evidence for the existence of God is cause and effect. Simply stated, every effect has a cause. For example, if you found a dime on the sidewalk, you would conclude that someone dropped it there. If you drove in a neighborhood and saw a new home, you would conclude that someone built it.

Since every effect has a cause, there must be a first uncaused cause that started everything. If not, the argument deteriorates into an infinite, meaningless regression. In other words, if there is no first uncaused cause, the beginning can never be found. If the beginning is never found, there is no starting point from which to come forward to the present. This would mean the present could not exist. If the present does not exist, we do not exist. But there is a present, and we do exist! Therefore, there had to be a beginning. Everything, then, was triggered by the uncaused-cause. We call this uncaused-cause, God.

Put another way, we live in a time-space-matter continuum. In order for each of these to exist in the present, they had to have a beginning. For example, if matter did not have a beginning, then a person would go back forever trying to find its origin. If he went back forever, there would be no starting point from which to come forward to the present. This would mean matter could not exist in the present. But matter does exist in the present, thus making it impossible for matter to be eternal. Matter then, must have a beginning. The same is true for time and space. Both must have a beginning in order to exist in the present. These are mind-stretching concepts, but logically speaking, they must be true.

Take a few moments to study Figure F-1 as you read the next several paragraphs.

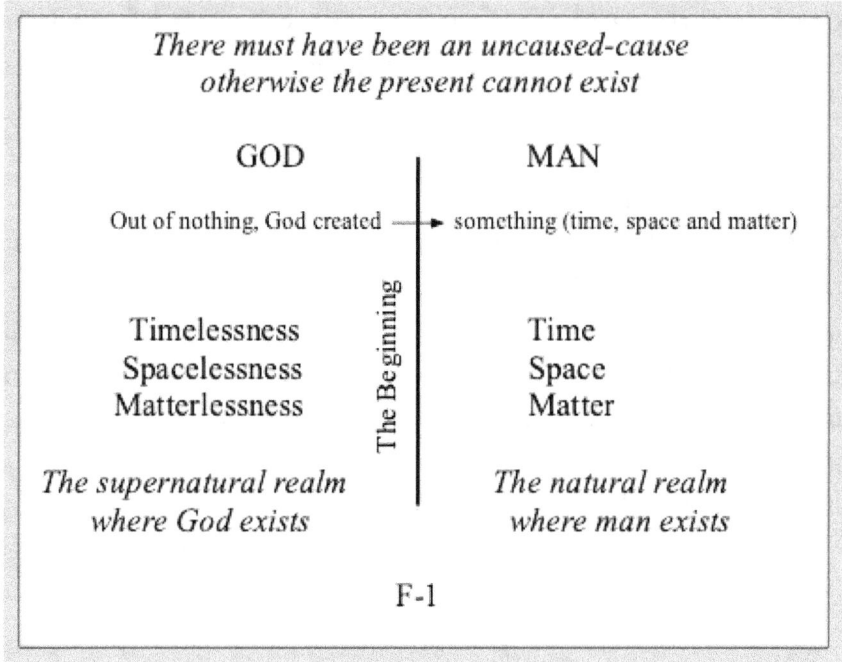

F-1

Based on the preceding evidence that time, space, and matter all had a beginning, there had to be a timeless-spaceless-matterless state before they began. In F-1, the portion to the right of the beginning might be termed 'The Natural State' in which time, space, and matter exist. The portion to the left of the beginning might be called 'The Supernatural State' – super meaning above nature.

Although man exists in the natural state, only God and other supernatural beings like angels can exist in the supernatural state.

This agrees with the Bible because it teaches that God and angels are spirits. Both God and angels can take on physical form, but they are spirits in their essence. A spirit does not have flesh and bones and is not bound by time, space or matter.

In F-1, something (time, space, and matter) comes out of nothing (timelessness, spacelessness, and matterlessness). Interestingly, this is exactly what the Bible teaches: *In the beginning God created the heavens and the earth* (Genesis 1:1). The word for create is the Hebrew word 'bara' (Hebrew is the original language of the Old Testament). It means to create something out of nothing. God said, *Let there be light, and there was light* (Genesis 1:3). He spoke things into existence.

Some people argue, "In order for God to exist, He, too, must have a beginning." This, however, is faulty reasoning. When the beginning line (Shown in Figure F-1) is crossed from the natural to the supernatural state, human logic and laws no longer apply. In our finite minds, it is impossible to completely understand the infinite. The Bible says God's ways are higher than our ways and His thoughts higher than our thoughts (Isaiah 55:8,9).

The argument from cause and effect is strong evidence for God's existence.

3. Complexity of Life

The world around us is incredibly complex. When we look at it closely, we should realize it never could have come about by random processes.

Consider the human body. It has a circulatory system, digestive system, nervous system, muscular/skeletal system, immune system, hormonal system, reproductive system, respiratory system, heating and cooling systems, balance system... brain, heart, and lungs... sense of smell, touch, sight, hearing, and taste... skin and speech, and the list goes on. All of these work in amazing harmony. Indeed, we do not realize how incredibly complex we are until something goes wrong. For anyone to believe this intricate myriad of interrelated systems and processes evolved through random mutations requires much more faith than believing in God.

Many folks believe that evolution happened through small mutative changes over a long period of time. The problem with this argument is that at least 99.9% of all mutations are harmful, causing things to deteriorate rather than improve. For example, to create something as intricate as a human eye with its lens, muscles, optic nerve, cones, cornea, blood supply, eyelid, eyelashes, eyebrows, depth-perception (two eyes are needed for this) and tear ducts would take literally millions of positive mutations each one needing to be passed on to the next generation. Also, a center in the brain would have to develop to interpret the information received through the optic nerve, somehow make sense of it, and communicate it to the rest of the body. The statistical possibility of this happening is essentially zero.

In addition, until an eye was fully formed, it would be of no advantage to the creature that possessed it. In fact, it would be a hindrance and lessen a creature's chance of survival, thus undermining the idea of natural selection. There are myriads of books that discuss the whole evolution-creation debate in much more depth. This issue will be looked at in greater depth later on in the Answers Course.

Suffice it to say, King David in the Bible was correct when he said in Psalm 139:14, *I will give thanks to Thee, for I am fearfully and wonderfully made; wonderful are Thy works, and my soul knows it very well.* The human body is fearfully and wonderfully made. The One who made it is to be reverently respected (feared) because He possesses awesome power far greater than humans.

Listen also to the words from the Bible found in Romans 1:20: *For since the creation of the world His (God's) invisible attributes, His eternal power and divine nature, have been clearly seen, being understood through what has been made, so that they are without excuse.* Simply stated, people who look at the complex world all around them and still reject God will be without excuse when they stand before Him at judgment.

4. Common Moral Standards

The fourth evidence for God's existence is common moral standards. Every society has a set of moral standards that condemns things like murder, adultery, stealing, cheating, and oppression. Even in countries where power-hungry political leaders are in control, people long for human freedom and fair treatment.

Why do people everywhere have these common standards even though many have never heard the Ten Commandments? The most reasonable explanation is that God placed them in their hearts. Again, this is what the Bible teaches. Because man is made in the moral image of God, he has an inherent awareness of right and wrong. Although he can numb his conscience through repeated sin, he still knows God's basic standards. If evolution were true, man's moral standards would be as varied as the colors of the rainbow, but they are not.

Some people argue, "I see no problem with adultery or things like stealing." This argument falls apart, however, when someone steals from them or commits adultery with their spouse. They are then quick to scream foul. Universal moral standards are strong evidence for God's existence.

5. Character and Emotions

The fifth evidence for God's existence is character and emotions. Not only do humans have a universal moral code of right and wrong, but they also have a common code of noble character traits. Qualities such as boldness, courage, endurance, sensitivity, patience, self-discipline, self-control, forgiveness, and generosity are looked upon as laudable. Traits such as slothfulness, stinginess, arrogance, insensitivity, selfishness, and impatience are considered undesirable. Who placed the value of these qualities in the heart of humans? The most reasonable answer is, "God did!"

The same is true of emotions. It is impossible to weigh ten pounds of anger, two ounces of loneliness, or a gallon of joy. It might be accurately said that emotions have a strong connection to the supernatural. We can't see, taste, or weigh them, but they are every bit as real as things in the physical world. A person's broken leg may heal in eight weeks, but a broken heart may take years.

Some people argue that emotions are associated with chemical reactions in the body. Although this is true, these chemical reactions were placed there by God as His means of bringing emotions into the physical realm.

Character and emotions are powerful evidence for God's existence.

6. Colors

Another evidence for God's existence is colors. Although this may sound a bit strange, consider the following. The color of an object is based on the wavelengths of light it absorbs and reflects. A red object absorbs all colors but red, which it reflects. The same is true of green, blue, yellow, and every color except black and white. Black is the only color that absorbs all colors. White is the only color that reflects all colors.

In one sense, color is a phenomenon that seems to be in the supernatural realm because there is no way to describe it accurately to a person who cannot see. If a rough or smooth, hot or cold, big or small object is given to a blind person, he can understand its properties by touch. On the other hand, he cannot understand color without seeing it. A red object feels the same as a blue one. A black one feels identical to a white one.

For a moment, picture yourself talking to a blind person. Try describing the color blue. You might say, "Blue is like the sky." But the sky can also be red. You might say, "Blue is the color of water." But brown water would feel the same. Although it is possible to describe objects that are a certain color, it is impossible to describe them adequately to a person who has no visual reference. Any explanation falls short. Colors thus point to the supernatural realm and the existence of God.

7. Continuity of the Bible

A seventh evidence for God's existence is the continuity of the Bible.

If forty different authors, over the next thousand plus years, who knew little about each other, were given the task of writing chapters for a book on religion, do you think there would be any contradictions in the writing? Absolutely! Yet the Bible was written in precisely the same manner and done so with perfect harmony.

Someone said about the Bible, "If humans would write such a book, they could not. And if they could write such a book, they would not." This statement basically means that if people set out to write the Bible, they could not do it because it is too perfect. It flows together too well. On the other hand, if people could write the Bible, they would not because its godly values and tone point to the holiness of God and the sinfulness of mankind. In essence by writing such a book, men would be condemning themselves. This flies in the face of human nature. Humans aren't in the habit of self-condemnation but instead self-justification.

Every religious book (except the Bible) that men have written has men reaching up to God through good works, trying to earn salvation. The Bible shows just the opposite: sinful men unable to reach God through their own efforts, needing to rely on God's graciousness to reach down to them in their sinfulness. The very tone of the Bible does not fit human authorship.

If mankind is incapable of writing the Bible, how did it get written? The best explanation is that God inspired and guided humans in its writing. He revealed His truth to them, and they spoke it or wrote it down. This is precisely what the Bible teaches (2 Timothy 3:16, 2 Peter 1:21).

8. Completed (fulfilled) Prophecy

Another aspect of the Bible that points to Divine authorship is fulfilled Bible prophecy. Scholars have identified approximately 300 specific prophecies about Christ. Most were fulfilled at His first coming, and some have yet to be fulfilled at His second coming. Many of the prophecies were written hundreds of years before Jesus came to earth. Most of the prophecies are extremely specific. Two such prophecies are that Christ would be born of a virgin (Isaiah 7:14) and die the death of crucifixion (Psalm 22:16). Not only is a virgin birth miraculous, but crucifixion was not a form of capital punishment at the time the prophecy was written.

It is one thing to prophesy that a person will die. All of us will die! It is something else to prophesy how a person will die, especially when that form of death is not being used at the time the prediction is made. Statistically speaking, the chance of fulfilling 300 specific prophecies without supernatural intervention is zero!

The Bible and its fulfilled prophecies are strong evidence for God's existence. The entire second chapter of the Answers Course addresses the question of the Bible's origin.

9. Comfort and Conviction of the Holy Spirit

A ninth evidence for God's existence is the comfort and conviction of the Holy Spirit. The Holy Spirit is part of the Trinity of God: Father, Son, and Holy Spirit. The Bible teaches that the Holy Spirit indwells every Christian and brings comfort and conviction. He comforts believers during difficult times.

He brings conviction by working in a person's conscience to give him a heightened awareness of right and wrong.

Listen to 1 John 4:13, *By this we know that we abide in Him and He in us, because He has given us of His Spirit.* When a person comes to Jesus Christ and asks Him to be Lord and Savior, the Holy Spirit takes up residence in his body. 1 Corinthians 6:19,20 reads, *Or do you not know that your body is a temple of the Holy Spirit who is in you, whom you have from God, and that you are not your own. For you have been bought with a price: therefore, glorify God in your body.*

It is one thing to say the Bible teaches that the Holy Spirit indwells all believers. This proves nothing. It is quite another to experience first-hand the comfort and conviction of the indwelling Spirit. Amazingly, Christians everywhere have similar experiences regarding the Spirit's ministry and work in their lives. Here are some things I and other Christians have personally experienced many times:

- Comfort and peace in the midst of difficulty. When I have faced things like major surgery, I have gone in with a new sense of peace since becoming a Christian. I know that even if I don't make it through surgery, I belong to God.

- A new sensitivity to sin. Things that used not to bother me, like swearing and crude jokes, have become repulsive. As one person put it, "I can't get into a good sin without the Holy Spirit reminding me that I am a Christian."
- A new love and concern for people. Since becoming a Christian, I find that I care more about others and want to help them if I can.
- Inner promptings to do things for God's kingdom like giving of my resources to help others in need.
- A new understanding of spiritual things. The Bible has taken on new meaning and seems much more understandable when I read it.

The closer a person walks with God, the more the Spirit's presence is felt. There is no other way to explain these things than to say, "The Holy Spirit really indwells believers and ministers to them."

10. Changed Lives

Another marvelous evidence of God's existence is changed lives. This is simply the natural result of the indwelling Holy Spirit. To me, it is incredible to see what God can do with lives yielded to Him.

I vividly remember being in church one evening when a couple gave their testimony. They were happy people, but I soon learned this had not always been the case. Only two years earlier, the husband had an alcohol problem, and the marriage was on the rocks. The husband shared how he and his wife were constantly in verbal battles. Then, through a neighbor's sharing, the wife became a Christian. As a new believer, she decided not to take part in the hurtful verbal exchanges in their home. This infuriated her husband. One evening, after too many drinks, he exploded. Amidst his screaming and her silence, he picked up a butcher knife and threatened to kill her. Her response was, "Do what you will, but I won't fight with you anymore." She said the tears welled up in her eyes as she stood frozen in place, waiting for the piercing pain of the blade. The seconds seemed like eternity. In frustration, her husband finally threw the knife at the wall. It bounced off of cabinet doors as it ricocheted around the kitchen. He stormed out of the room, and his wife stood physically unharmed.

Not knowing how to handle his wife, the husband began avoiding her. Amidst this rejection, she silently continued her wifely duties, prayed for her husband, and met with her neighbor, who helped her grow as a Christian.

Through a series of events, sparked by his wife's silent witness and changed life, the husband finally gave his heart to Christ. Soon, he stopped drinking. Two years later, he was holding his wife's hand and giving a personal testimony in church about how Christ had changed his life and saved their marriage. It was a powerful evening.

How does one explain such stories? The most logical explanation is God's power changing the lives of people! I could tell many such stories and perhaps you could, too. They are strong evidence for God's existence.

11. Christ's Life, Death, and Resurrection

Perhaps the most powerful evidence for God's existence is the life, death and resurrection of Jesus Christ. The Bible states that

Jesus was born of a virgin, which in itself is a miracle. It also states that during His life He performed many amazing miracles. But what is arguably the most amazing thing about Jesus is His resurrection. The Bible states that He physically rose from the dead. 1 Corinthians 15:14 states, *And if Christ has not been raised, then our preaching is vain, your faith also is vain.* This verse makes it clear that Jesus Christ's resurrection is the crux of Christianity. If He actually rose from the dead, He can promise eternal life to others. If He did not rise, Christianity has no real authority.

Even today with all our amazing technology, no one comes back from the dead after three days! If God wanted to prove Christ was His Son, and Christianity was true, a real resurrection would be a great way to do it. This is precisely what God did. Chapter four in the Answers Course covers in detail the evidence for Christ's resurrection.

The life, death, and resurrection of Christ are historic facts. There are many convincing arguments to illustrate this. Regarding Christ's life, our whole Western calendar revolves around Him. The key holidays of Christmas and Easter are about Him. Christmas commemorates Christ's birth, while Easter celebrates His resurrection.

If Jesus had not lived, there is no way He could have become our calendar's focus. Even the dating system of the western calendar is based on Jesus. The year AD 2004 means 2004 years since the birth of Christ. Some people think AD means After Death. Actually, it is two Latin words Anno Domini, meaning in the year of our Lord, dated from Christ's birth. BC means Before Christ. If AD meant after death (which it does not), the 33 years that Jesus lived on this earth would be lost from the calendar. Having BC mean before Christ, and AD mean in the year of our Lord (dated from his birth), no years are lost.

In recent days, there is a very deliberate attempt by those who oppose Christianity to remove anything Christian from society. One rather covert way has been by changing the calendar's dating system. Rather than BC meaning before Christ, writers have changed dates in many new textbooks to read BCE, defined as 'Before the Common Era.' Unsuspecting readers and school children are caught totally unaware. Rather than having a calendar that for 2,000 years revolved around the central figure of Western civilization, Jesus Christ, many are trying to have it revolve around nothing.

Through His resurrection, Jesus did something that no other man has done before or since. He predicted his own death and resurrection, and then fulfilled both predictions.

Today, medical personnel may revive someone whose heart has stopped for a few minutes, but no one, except God, can revive someone who has been dead for three days. That is precisely what He did with Jesus.

SUMMARY

There is strong evidence for God's existence from many areas:

1. Consciousness of God
2. Cause and effect
3. Complexity of life
4. Common moral standards
5. Character and emotions
6. Colors
7. Continuity of the Bible
8. Completed (fulfilled) prophecy
9. Comfort and conviction of the Holy Spirit
10. Changed lives

11. Christ's life, death, and resurrection

Does this evidence give people good reasons to believe in the existence of God? Absolutely! Although belief in God requires faith, it is certainly not blind faith. All the evidence, when taken together, is rather overwhelming. God exists!

DISCUSSION QUESTIONS

DOES GOD EXIST?

1. Which of the arguments for God's existence seem strongest to you? Why?

2. Which of the arguments seem weak in your opinion? Why?

3. What reasons do some folks give for why they believe in God? Are these good reasons? What, in your opinion, is a valid reason?

4. Would a loving God require people to have blind faith regarding His existence? Explain.

5. What is the argument presented in this study against being an atheist?

6. What other evidence can you think of for the existence of God?

7. Briefly summarize the arguments for God's existence.

   - Consciousness of God

   - Cause and effect

   - Complexity of life

   - Common moral standards

   -Character and emotions

- Colors

-Continuity of the Bible

-Completed (fulfilled) prophecy

-Comfort and conviction of the Holy Spirit

-Changed lives

-Christ's life, death, and resurrection

8. How has this chapter affected your belief in the existence of God?

CHAPTER

TWO

IS THE BIBLE GOD'S WORD?

THE RELEVANCE OF DIVINE AUTHORSHIP

Does it really matter whether or not the Bible's author is God? Absolutely! Besides the question "Does God exist?" there are few more basic religious questions than "Is the Bible the Word of God?" If it is not His Word, it can be ignored, or at best, referred to for the history of the Jewish people. If it is God's Word, it needs to be given the honor and attention it deserves. There are no other options. The Bible is either God's Word, requiring great devotion, or it can be put on the shelf and forgotten.

THE EVIDENCE FOR DIVINE AUTHORSHIP

1. Claims in the Bible

The first evidence for divine authorship is found in the pages of the Bible itself. It claims to be God's Word. Although this is not conclusive evidence, it certainly indicates the position of the writers on the subject.

There are numerous places in the Old Testament that make this claim. Examples are Exodus 20:1, Numbers 36:13, 1 Samuel 3:11, and Isaiah 1:2. Phrases similar to *"thus saith the Lord"* are used over 3,800 times in the Old Testament.[1]

Another interesting phenomenon is found in passages that seem to equate Scripture with God Himself. Romans 9:17 states, *For the Scripture says to Pharaoh, 'For this very purpose I raised you up, to demonstrate My power in you, and that My name might be proclaimed throughout the whole earth.'* This passage refers back to Exodus 9:13-16 in the Old Testament in which Moses was told to relay this message to Pharaoh. The equating of Scripture and God is really just an acknowledgement that Scripture is God's Word. When Scripture talks, God talks.

Many of the prophets in the Old Testament considered the words of former prophets to be the Word of God. Ezra recognized the divine authority of Jeremiah's writings in Ezra 1:1. In Zechariah 7:12, the prophet Zechariah recognized the divine nature of the writings of all the former prophets. Similar reference is made in Nehemiah 9:30.

Some people argue that although the Old Testament contains numerous passages claiming to be God's Word, there is no claim the entire Old Testament is God's Word. The Apostle Paul dispels this argument in 2 Timothy 3:16 in the New Testament **All Scripture is inspired by God** *and profitable for teaching, for reproof, for correction, for training in righteousness; that the man of God may be adequate, equipped for every good work.*

When Paul refers to Scripture, he means the entire Old

1. William Evans, *The Greatest Doctrines of The Bible,* (Bibliotech Press, 2019), 203.

Testament. He says it is literally the breath of God. The word inspired means God-breathed.

In 2 Peter 1:20-21, the apostle Peter also viewed the Old Testament writings as God-breathed, *But know this first of all, that no prophecy of Scripture is a matter of one's own interpretation, **for no prophecy was ever made by an act of human will, but men moved by the Holy Spirit spoke from God.***

Regarding the authorship of the New Testament, Peter refers to Paul's writings as Scripture in 2 Peter 3:14-16. In 1 Timothy 5:18, Paul quotes both Deuteronomy 25:4 and Luke 10:7 and refers to them as Scripture.

Jesus told the disciples that the Holy Spirit would bring to their remembrance all things He had said and would guide them into all truth (John 14:26 and John 16:13).

Just like the Old Testament, the New Testament claims to be the Word of God. Indeed, it is clear the entire Bible makes this claim! If this claim is false, the Bible is a deceptive piece of literature that has misled untold millions who have followed its teachings. If, on the other hand, this claim is true, the Bible deserves our truest respect and utmost devotion.

2. Christ's Endorsement

The second evidence for the Bible's divine authorship is Christ's endorsement. He viewed it as God's Word. In Matthew 22:29, He confronted the Sadducees, telling them they did not understand the Scriptures. By using the word Scriptures, Jesus meant the Old Testament.

In Matthew 21:42, Christ asked the Pharisees, *Did you never read the Scriptures?* Here again, Jesus referred to the Old Testament as having final authority as God's Word. In Matthew 26:56, when Jesus was betrayed, He referred to the Old Testament when He said, *But all this has taken place to fulfill the Scriptures of the prophets.* In John 10:35, Jesus equated "the Word of God" with "Scripture." He went on to say that *Scripture cannot be broken.*

Jesus also referred to the Old Testament as *the Law and the Prophets* in Luke 16:16. In verse 17, Jesus went on to say, *But it is easier for heaven and earth to pass away than for one stroke of a letter of the Law to fail.* He said the same thing in Matthew 5:17,18. In addition, when Jesus was tempted, He referred to the Old Testament as having divine authority (Matthew 4:1-12).

If Jesus is God's Son (which many believe He is), and if He referred to the Scriptures as God's inspired Word (which He certainly did), then the Bible must be precisely what He claimed it to be!

3. Canonization of Scripture

The third evidence supporting the claim that the Bible is God's Word is its canonization. The word canon comes from the Greek word 'kanon,' meaning ruler, staff, or measuring rod. The Greek word undoubtedly came from the Hebrew word 'kaneh' (reed), that was an Old Testament term used for measuring rod.[2]

Canonization may be defined as the process men used in recognizing which writings were God's Word by whether or not they measured up to a certain standard. If the writings measured up, they were included in the Canon of Scripture. If they did not measure up, they were rejected.

It must be stressed that men did not determine which writings belonged in the Bible as God's Word; they simply recognized or

---

2. *Geisler and Nix, A General Introduction To The Bible (Moody Press, 1968),* 127.

discovered which ones were already God's Word. The writings were His Word at the time of writing, not at the point of canonization.

Some people say canonization is a non-argument for the Bible being God's Word because the standard was determined by men. Others maintain the way the standard was set and canonization done is strong evidence for the Bible being God's Word.

With these two views in mind, let's examine the standard. First, the standard was NOT based on any of the following: the age of a book, whether or not it was written in the Hebrew language, whether it agreed with the Torah (the law of Moses), or whether it had religious value. There were some ancient writings not included in the canon. There were Hebrew writings that were not included in the canon. There were books that agreed with the Torah that were not included in the canon. It is important to note no books or writings disagreeing with the Torah were included. Just because a book agreed with the Torah was no guarantee it would be included in the canon. Also, some books having apparent religious value were not included in the canon because they did not measure up to certain parts of the standard.[3]

Canonization of the Old Testament was accepted by the Jews as the Word of God before the time of Christ, probably between 400 and 200 BC. The Jews commonly referred to this literature as "The Law, the Prophets, and the Writings." Some scholars suggest they had this three-fold division to identify whether the author was a prophet, priest, prince, or king used by God to give a prophetic utterance.[4]

Before, during, and after the time of Christ, there was a proliferation of religious writings. Early church leaders became increasingly concerned about how to identify which writings were

---

3. 3. *Ibid., p. 130-133.*
4. *Ibid., p. 161.*

truly from God and which were the work of men. This search led to much discussion, debate, and some disagreement. Through a process spanning the first four centuries AD, the books of the canon of Scripture were identified. This process included not only the discussion and interaction of the apostles and other early church leaders but also four important councils: the Council of Nicea (AD 325-340), the Council of Hippo (AD 393), and two Councils of Carthage (AD 397 and AD 419).

Other stimuli also contributed to the canonization of Scripture. One was the *need* of the 1st Century church. Early Christians needed to know what books could provide an authoritative norm for faith and practice. Another stimulus was heresy. There were people like Marcion, who rejected certain sections of the New Testament that most others considered to be God's Word. Without an approved canon, it was hard for early church members to know whom to believe. A third stimulus was missions. As Christian missionaries spread the gospel, they needed to know which writings were God's Word so they could confidently give them to their new converts. Persecution was also a clear incentive for canonization. The Roman emperor Diocletian ordered the burning of Scriptures and the persecution of Christians in approximately AD 302/3. Christians who hid religious writings wanted to know which writings were worth protecting with their lives.[5]

In the canonization process, five principles were used for recognizing God's Word. A number of different Councils were held to discuss these principles and their application. By the end of the councils, the books in our current Bible had been identified and confirmed.

---

5. *Ibid., p. 180.*

The principles may be summarized by the following words: authoritative, apostolic (prophetic), authentic, active (dynamic), and accepted (received). Let's look at these one at a time.[6]

a. **Authoritative** - Authoritative meant that a writing had the authority of God. This served as the first and foremost principle in recognizing a writing's canonicity. It was also a logical presupposition of any Word of God. By God's very nature, His Word is authoritative. The Councils used certain questions to determine the authority of a particular writing. For example, does the writing speak with authority? Does the writer use a phrase like, *"Thus saith the Lord"*? Does it have an implicit authority commanding the attention of its readers? This principle easily identified the works of the prophets. Other writings were easily rejected. Some books, like Esther, required closer examination.

b. **Apostolic** (Prophetic) - Apostolic (or prophetic) meant that a writing was written by a man of God. It was only logical the Word of God would come through a man of God. In the case of New Testament writings, the Councils asked, "Were these writings written by an apostle or a close associate of an apostle?" Although Luke, the author of Luke and Acts, was not an apostle, he was a close associate of both Peter and Paul. The books of Luke and Acts, thus, measured up to this standard.

c. **Authentic** - Authentic meant a writing that told the truth about God and man and remained consistent with writings already recognized to be God's Word. This quality of God's Word also comes from the logical

---

6. *Ibid., p. 138.*

premise God does not lie, and His Word is consistent. Agreement with the rest of God's Word did not make a writing automatically canonical, but disagreement definitely made it non-canonical.

d. **Active** (Dynamic) - Active meant a writing that had the power of God to change lives. Early church fathers believed God's Word was accurately described as *living and active* in Hebrews 4:12. If a writing had God as its source, a person who obeyed its message would see his life change for the good.

e. **Accepted** - Accepted meant the writing or book had been generally accepted by God's people. Christ stated His sheep recognize His voice. Thus, generally speaking, Christians would recognize and accept writing that was truly from God

In summary, if a writing was clearly authoritative (it claimed to be His Word and contained no errors in history or theology), the rest of the principles could be essentially assumed. Since it was not always easy to determine the clear authority of a writing, the other principles became extremely helpful. The first three principles; authoritative, apostolic, and authentic, were used explicitly on all books, while the last two principles, active and accepted, were used implicitly. In other words, if a writing measured up in the first three areas, the last two were essentially a given. If any of the first three were unclear, the last two helped clear the air. Every book the Council identified as canonical had to measure up to all five principles at least implicitly. Thus, the canon of Scripture was identified.

For a more complete look at the area of canonization, the book *A General Introduction to The Bible* by Norman L. Geisler and William E. Nix (1968, Moody Press) is extremely helpful. If you cannot find this book in your local library, you can certainly order it online through www.Christianbook.com (Christian Book Distributors).

4. Copying Accuracy of Old Testament Documents

The fourth evidence for the Bible being God's Word is what might be called copying accuracy. This deals with the way the Bible has been handed down through the generations.

Regarding the Old Testament, it was the job of scribes to copy the sacred writings of the Jews. They had meticulous rules governing their task. Writings could only be done on special animal skins. Every skin had to be marked off with a certain number of columns that had to stay consistent throughout the entire document. Each column consisted of exactly 30 letters. Each skin had to have between 48 and 60 lines. The ink had to be black, and the scribe could write nothing from memory. He had to meticulously copy each stroke after he looked back at the original. A precise distance of one hair's breadth between every consonant and a specific distance between sections and books also had to occur. Scribes were required to sit in full Jewish dress and not begin to write the name of God with a pen that had been just dipped in ink. If, while writing the name of God, the scribe was interrupted by even a king, he was to ignore that person until after he had completely written the name. Scribes methodically counted lines and letters, and if even one error was found, the new manuscript was destroyed, and the whole process restarted.[7]

Why did the Jews have such rigid requirements for making copies of their sacred writings? Their reverence for God demanded

---

7. *Ibid., p. 241, 252.*

it! Also they wanted God's Word to be handed down from one generation to the next without change or perversion.

Unfortunately, old Hebrew manuscripts are rare. The reasons for this are many. The skins on which the writing was done have decayed over time. The wanderings of the Jews are another reason. As they constantly moved through the years, it was difficult to preserve ancient writings. Also, Jerusalem was conquered 47 times between 1800 BC and AD 1948. These wars took their toll on the temple where the writings were kept. It was often plundered. In addition, the scribes methodical destruction of worn manuscripts eliminated the oldest documents. Finally, the standardization of Hebrew in the fifth and sixth centuries led to the disposal of many older documents. Up until 1947, the oldest Hebrew manuscripts available only dated back to the tenth century AD. Even with the incredibly accurate tradition of the scribes for copying text, skeptics still claimed the Old Testament probably had many changes from the original writings. The discovery of the Dead Sea Scrolls in 1947 changed the minds of many of these skeptics. While pursuing a lost goat 7.5 miles south of Jericho, an Arab shepherd boy discovered a cave containing jars with several leather scrolls. Upon further investigation, several more caves were discovered, with many more writings. These writings had belonged to a Jewish sect known as the Essenes, who lived during the time of Christ. The scrolls contained much of the Old Testament. These writings provided evidence over one thousand years older than any previous writings. When they were compared to the manuscripts from the tenth century AD, there were virtually no changes! This confirmed the fact, what we have today is indeed what was written from the very beginning.[8]

8. Ibid., p. 250-255.

Why was the Old Testament so accurately preserved? Many people believe it was the hand of God protecting His Word.

5. Correlation of New Testament Documents

The vast number and precise correlation of ancient New Testament documents is amazing and can only be adequately accounted for by divine intervention and protection. Other ancient historic documents are not nearly as plentiful. The Iliad of Homer was reconstructed from 643 manuscripts. Caesar's Gallic Wars have only nine or ten remaining good manuscripts. Only 20 manuscripts are available for Livy's History of Rome. Conversely, approximately 3,000 Greek manuscripts remain of parts of the New Testament dating from as far back as the second century. In addition, the early church fathers of the second and third centuries quoted various parts of the New Testament some 36,000 times. Even if there were no Greek manuscripts available, the entire New Testament, except for eleven verses, could be completely reconstructed from these quotations.

The 9,000 manuscripts containing parts of ancient and medieval versions of the Old and New Testaments also serve as another source for reconstructing the New Testament. The service books, known as Lectionaries, used in early churches also helped in the reconstruction of the New Testament. At least 2,000 of these have survived through the ages.

Another important factor about ancient manuscripts is the amount of time between their writing and the events they describe. Except for the New Testament, other ancient manuscripts postdate the events they describe by as much as 1,000 years. In the case of the New Testament, the earliest documents date within a generation of the time of Christ and many within 100-200 years.

When these documents are compared and correlated, researchers find a number of variant readings partly because the copying practices for the New Testament were not nearly as stringent as those for the Old. However, most of the variants are trivialities and simply a matter of spelling or style.

To better understand these variants, consider the following information. The New Testament was originally written in individual capital Greek letters known as uncials. No word divisions or punctuation were used. Words were simply strung together. Later, for ease of writing, scribes used lower case letters (miniscules) and cursive style. Still later, they divided words and added punctuation. This is where many of the variants came into play. The science of Textual Criticism can easily explain these variants. Most of them have to do with spelling and style changes of the transcribers.

A transcriber trying to determine how to divide the following letters:

GODISNOWHERE could either divide it as GOD IS NOW HERE or as GOD IS NOWHERE. Other variants had to do with transposers accidentally leaving out a word or line as they copied a document. For an in-depth discussion of the science of Textual Criticism and how it applies to the New Testament Documents, the book *A General Introduction To The New Testament* by Geisler and Nix, Chapter 26, is invaluable.

When all the variant readings of the New Testament are compared and correlated, many textual critics believe we can be

99.9% sure what we have today is what the original writers wrote. It must be said the variants pose no problems with doctrinal issues.[9]

What can account for the vast number of New Testament Documents that are available compared to other ancient writings? What can account for their incredible agreement? The only reasonable explanation is God is their ultimate author and preserver.

6. Choice of Biblical Languages

Another evidence for the Bible being God's Word is found in the original languages of the Bible. The primary languages are Hebrew in the Old Testament and Greek in the New Testament.

It is indeed interesting that these are the two primary languages of the Bible. Hebrew is a pictorial language appealing to the senses and heart and is a perfect choice for a biography of the Jewish people. Since the Old Testament was given specifically to the Jews, it is also appropriate it be written in their own language.

On the other hand, the New Testament is written in Greek. Greek is a very precise language appealing primarily to the mind. This is the perfect language for explaining God's great doctrines and truths.

An example of the exactness of the Greek language is found in the word "love." In English, people say, "I love my wife," "I love Pepsi Cola," or "I love to play tennis." But what does love really mean? To a foreigner. it would indeed be confusing. Greek, on the other hand, has several words for love. One word is 'agape.' This is a selfless love that puts others first. In Greek, the meaning of Ephesians 5:25 is clear, *"Husbands love [agape] your wives as Christ loved the church."*

---

9. Ibid., p. 358-366.

Greek was also the universal language of its day. Since God intended to spread His truth to the whole world, Greek was the ideal language to use. Hebrew, on the other hand, was the perfect language to communicate God's Word to a specific people, the Jews.

God has communicated to people in many ways throughout history. He used angels, visions, dreams, casting lots, conscience, creation, audible voice, the Holy Spirit, and miracles. Although these have their place, God also wanted to communicate in a way that would reach a great number of people in a clear and transferable way. He did this through writing. The Hebrew and Greek languages were His perfect vehicles.

It seems improbable these languages just happened to be the ones available when God decided to communicate. It is more reasonable that God prepared them ahead of time to fit into His eternal plan.[10]

7. Climate Conditions in Israel

One factor allowing many biblical documents to survive through the centuries was the dry climate of the Holy Land. If God wanted to preserve certain writings, it seems logical He would place them in a location conducive to their survival. If the Dead Sea Scrolls, found in Israel's desert, had been buried in a humid area like the Southeastern United States, they would have decomposed long ago.

Why did the Bible originate in an area with such a dry climate? Was it chance? I believe it was God's plan.

. . .

10. Ibid., p. 211-234.

8. Complete Unity of the Bible

A unique characteristic of the Bible is its complete unity. Although it was written over a period of 1,500 years by 40 different authors from various backgrounds, it has a single theme – God's wonderful plan of salvation. Certainly. the canonization process helped ensure this unity. but the unity is still amazing.

Today, imagine taking 40 people and asking them to write a unified document on a particular subject. Unless they could talk extensively with each other, the prospects of overall unity would be quite slim. Even if they talked to one another, they would undoubtedly have differences of opinion, making writing such a document nearly impossible.

What can account for the Bible's incredible unity? Nothing short of divine inspiration!

9. Concise Prophecies, and Their Fulfillment

One of the most amazing evidences for divine authorship of the Bible is prophecy within its pages. The Bible contains many predictions made long before the events they describe. These events were subsequently fulfilled in precise detail. One specific example concerns the city of Tyre (Ezekiel 26). This prophecy contains eight specific predictions:

1. The city would be destroyed by more than one nation (v4).
2. The place where it stood would be wiped clean (vv4,14).
3. It would become a place for spreading nets (vv5, 14).
4. The inhabitants would be slain by the sword (v6).
5. Nebuchadnezzar would be one of the conquerors (vv7-13).
6. The city would never be rebuilt (v14).

7. Other people would tremble at the destruction (vv15-18).
8. The original city would be brought down and covered by the sea (v19).

The incredible thing about this prophecy is it was made when Tyre was a thriving seaport city on the northern coast of Palestine. Part of the city was on the mainland and part on an island about one-half mile off-shore. Tyre's inhabitants, the Phoenicians, were a strong, sea-going people greatly feared for their maritime power. In those days, with high walls and towers, the city was virtually impregnable.

In 586 BC, the king of Babylon, Nebuchadnezzar, laid siege to the city and finally conquered it thirteen years later. Although this siege destroyed the mainland portion of Tyre, many of the Phoenicians were able to escape to the island. Nebuchadnezzar was unable to capture the island. His conquest fulfilled some but not all of the prophecy. For over 200 years, the city of Tyre remained as Nebuchadnezzar left it.

Later, during Alexander the Great's conquests, the city was again attacked. Fearing the fleet of Tyre, Alexander's army laid siege to the area in 322 BC. Although he conquered some surrounding cities, his army was unable to take the island portion of Tyre. To finish the task, Alexander had his men scrape the ruins of the old city into the sea in order to build a causeway to the island. The idea worked, and Tyre was completely destroyed.

Other surrounding cities were so fearful of Alexander that they peacefully opened their gates to him.

Today, those who visit Tyre will find a barren, flat place where the city used to be. The original city lies under the sea as part of the causeway. Fishermen now use the place to spread their nets.

Although Tyre's original location still has springs, making it an ideal spot for reconstructing a new city, the site remains barren. All of the prophecy was thus completed.

There are many prophecies about the Jewish people as well. Perhaps the best-known prophecy concerns their return to their homeland. When the Jews were scattered shortly after the time of Christ, people thought the fulfillment of the prophecy predicting their return to Israel (Isaiah 11:11,12) was virtually impossible. Then, the miraculous happened. In 1948, following the close of World War II, Israel once again became a nation after a long 2,000-year exile.

Besides these prophecies, there are approximately 300 more about Christ in the Old Testament, most of which were fulfilled at His first coming. Some will be fulfilled at His second coming.

What can account for the incredibly precise biblical prophecies and their fulfillment? Again, the only adequate explanation is that the Bible is God's Word.

10. Capacity of the Bible to Survive

A tenth evidence for the Bible being the Word of God is its incredible capacity to survive. Throughout history, there have been many violent attacks against it, all to no avail. In AD 302-303, the Roman emperor, Diocletian, issued an imperial letter ordering the burning of churches and the destruction by fire of any Scriptures.

All people holding a church office would lose their civil rights, and any common people persisting in their Christian beliefs would lose their liberty. Obviously, the Bible withstood this aggressive assault.

In the 1700s, the famous French writer Voltaire predicted the Bible would pass into obscurity within a few years. Instead, it was Voltaire who has passed into relative obscurity.

Ironically, within 50 years of his death, the Geneva Bible Society was using Voltaire's printing press and home to print Bibles.[11]

11. Concise Scientific Data

Another evidence for the Bible being God's Word is its concise scientific data. Although the Bible is not primarily a scientific book, when it speaks about scientific things, it does so with amazing accuracy.

Throughout history, the scientific world has pointed an accusing finger at the Bible, saying it contains scientific errors. Time has shown science to be wrong and the Bible to be right.

One example has to do with the number of stars. Before the telescope was invented in the seventeenth century, astronomers believed there were approximately 1000 stars. Ptolemy put the number at 1,056. Tycho Brahe catalogued 777 stars. Kepler believed there were 1,005.

With the invention of the telescope, we now know there are more than 100 billion stars in our own galaxy and innumerable galaxies similar to our own. Jeremiah 33:22 reads *The host of heaven cannot be counted.* This statement refers to the number of stars in the heavens. It is interesting how long it took science to figure out what the Bible taught all along.

Another example comes from Job 26:7, which reads, *He hangs the earth on nothing.* The idea the earth hangs in space by itself sounds like scientific talk from the twenty-first century. Although scientists did not believe this until several hundred years ago, the Bible has taught it for thousands of years.

A third example is found in Isaiah 40:22. It reads, *It is He who sits above the circle of the earth...* The Hebrew word for circle is 'chuwg'

---

11. *Ibid., p. 123, 180, 181.*

which can be better translated as sphericity or roundness. Until modern times, people believed the world was flat. The Bible has always taught it is round. Again, it took time for science to see the truth.

A fifth example is found in Job 36:27,28 and Ecclesiastes 1:6-7. These passages explain the winds and the hydrologic processes of evaporation, condensation, and precipitation. This explanation is miraculous, considering these facts were not clearly understood until more recent times.

The sanitation and dietary laws of Moses found in Leviticus also show the scientific accuracy of the Bible. Certain foods were considered unclean, which the Jews were forbidden to eat. Other foods were considered clean and fit for human consumption. We now know there are good reasons for obeying these laws.

Also, God commanded the Jews to follow a certain procedure for disposing of human excrement (Deuteronomy 23:12-14). This procedure saved the Jews from many diseases that plagued other cultures. We now know these laws are scientifically prudent.[12]

In Genesis 1:1, the author says, *In the beginning God created the heavens and the earth.* The word for create is the word 'bara.' It means to create something out of nothing. The Bible clearly teaches that God spoke things into existence.

There have been many different scientific theories regarding origins. Many are now known to be false. One of the latest theories says everything began from an infinitesimal particle that exploded in a big bang. The question this raises is, "Where did the infinitesimal particle come from?" It seems this theory is another of man's futile attempts to explain the universe apart from an infinite God.

---

12. Henry M. Morris, The Bible and Modern Science, (Moody Press, 1968), 5-9.

If some scientists can believe the whole universe started from an infinitesimally small particle, why can they not believe it started from an infinite God who spoke things into existence? One reason seems to be that to admit there is a God would mean they would have to obey Him. Many would clearly rather maintain control of their own lives.

It is interesting to note that if the Bible had accommodated scientific thought for even the last hundred years, it would be obsolete today. Many scientific theories have been replaced by new ones. It seems the more we learn about science, the more we see the Bible's accuracy. As science continues to advance, I believe we will see even more biblical truth being confirmed.

The fact is, there are many scientists today who believe in God and see no contradiction between science and faith. They have followed in the footsteps of countless other scientists, including Albert Einstein. There are also organizations like the "Institute for Creation Research" (ICR) and "Answers In Genesis" (AIG) made up of scientists who believe in God. They continue to publish outstanding books that show the correlation between faith and science.

What can account for the scientific accuracy of the Bible? The only realistic explanation is divine authorship.

12. Confirmation of Historic Data by Archeology

Still another evidence for the Bible being God's Word is the confirmation of its historic data by archeology. In the past, the Bible has taken a beating from those who said it contained historical inaccuracies. Archeology continues to prove otherwise. Over the years, more and more of the persons, places, and events of the Bible have been confirmed.

One interesting example is found in 2 Kings 17:4, where it reads, *But the king of Assyria found conspiracy in Hoshea, and has sent messengers to So, king of Egypt...* Many historians have attacked this passage because history shows there never was a king by the name of "So" in Egypt. Now it is known the city of Sais, the capital of an Egyptian province, is where the king of Egypt resided at the time 2 Kings 17:4 was written. The text should read, *To So (Sais), to the king of Egypt.* Hosea, the king of Israel, was writing to the Egyptian king who lived in Sais, requesting his help in fighting the Assyrians. Instead of proving the Bible to be inaccurate, this passage confirms the Bible's accuracy.[13]

Although the confirmation of archeology does not prove the Bible is God's Word, it certainly is strong supporting evidence.

13. Changeless Truth

There is no doubt the Bible contains changeless truth. This is another evidence it is God's Word. It shows people how to have financial success, how to raise children, how to have a strong marriage, how to get along with others, how to avoid moral pitfalls, how to solve conflict, how to forgive people, how to have peace and joy, and a thousand other things. Those who have made the Bible their handbook for living have found great fulfillment.

What can account for the amazing principles found in the Bible? The only satisfactory explanation is the Bible is God's Word. God knows how we should operate and has given us the blueprint for life. When we follow His instructions, good things happen! When we don't, we suffer the consequences no matter how good our intentions.

---

13. Geisler and Nix, A General Introduction to the Bible (Moody Press, 1968), 253.

14. Capability to Change Lives

Not only is biblical truth changeless, it has the power to change lives. When Christ said, *Come to Me, all who are weary and heavy-laden, and I will give you rest* (Matthew 11:28), He meant it! When the apostle Paul stated, *Therefore if any man is in Christ, he is a new creature; the old things passed away; behold, new things have come* (2 Corinthians 5:17), this was more than wishful thinking.

The testimonies of those whose lives have been transformed by the power of God are endless. One such example is Pete. Pete was a playboy fireman who lived the motto, 'Let the good times roll.' In the midst of life-in-the-fast-lane, Pete found little fulfillment or meaning. Just the same, he was very negative toward Christianity and opposed anyone who questioned his self-indulgent lifestyle. Through a series of circumstances, Pete came to Christ and did a 180-degree turn in his attitudes. He became a great advocate of Christianity.

What can account for the millions like Pete who have had their lives radically changed for the good by the message of the gospel? The only acceptable explanation is the Bible is God's Word. Hebrews 4:12 states, *For the word of God is living and active and sharper than any two-edged sword and piercing as far as the division of soul and spirit, of both joints and marrow, and able to judge the thoughts and intentions of the heart.*

15. Common Appeal and Circulation of the Bible

The Bible has enjoyed the greatest common appeal and circulation of any book in the world. It is the greatest-selling book of all time. There are no close seconds. As other books have come and gone, the Bible continues to sell countless millions of copies each year. It is estimated that by 1932, more than 1.3 billion Bibles or portions of the Bible had been published.[14] Today the number is several times that figure.

In the era of modern technology when religion is out of vogue for some people, the Bible remains the number one best-seller.

What can account for the amazing appeal and circulation of the Bible? Again, the only clear explanation is the Bible is God's Word.

16. Code of Moral Standards

The Ten Commandments (Exodus 20) are also evidence the Bible is God's Word. They remain the bedrock for morality around the world. Sane people everywhere believe that murder, adultery, stealing, lying, and coveting are wrong. Even in cultures that claim to advocate different values, individuals are quick to scream foul when someone lies to them or commits adultery with their spouse.

What can account for the universal acceptance of the morality principles of the Ten Commandments? The logical explanation is God is their author.

17. The Church's Success

The existence of the church and its success is strong evidence the Bible is God's Word. The local church is the place where the principles of the Bible are systematically taught.

If the Bible is God's Word, it is logical an organization that followed its teachings would enjoy success. This is precisely what is happening with the Christian church.

Churches can be found in essentially every city of the Western world and many other areas as well. Even in places where

---

14. Ibid., p. 121.

Christianity is outlawed, underground churches exist and often thrive.

Although there are numerous religious cults in the world, none have enjoyed the long-term success of God's Christian church. Many of the cults claim to be Christian and even teach many Christian values, which may be one reason why people are drawn to them.

Islam is also growing rapidly, but it often makes converts through coercion. If faced with the choice of conversion or death, many people will choose to convert.

Becoming a Christian, on the other hand, is a choice people make based on their desire to give their lives to a God who loves them and sent His Son to die for them.

What can account for the worldwide success of the church? The logical explanation is that the Bible, from which the church gets its teachings, is the Word of God.

18. Comforting and Convicting Power of the Bible

The Bible's comforting and convicting power is clear evidence it is God's Word. Again, Hebrews 4:12 states, *For the Word of God is living and active and sharper than any two-edged sword, and piercing as far as the division of soul and spirit, of both joints and marrow, and able to judge the thoughts and intentions of the heart.*

Christians everywhere find the above-stated principle to be true. Scripture is living and active. It judges the thoughts and intentions of the heart.

The Bible not only convicts us of sin; it gives great comfort to those who read its pages. People who are anxious find inner peace as they read the Bible. The promises found in its pages have helped millions make it through difficult times. Someone has rightly said, "The Bible afflicts the comfortable and comforts the afflicted."

What can adequately account for the convicting and comforting power of the Bible? The clearest explanation is it is God's Word.

19. Conclusion of Alternate Appeal

An extremely interesting argument for the Bible being God's Word was first put forth by the famous preacher and theologian Charles Wesley. It is known as the argument from Alternate Appeal. It goes as follows:

The Bible must either be the invention of good men or angels, bad men or devils, or of God. It could not be the invention of good men or angels, for they neither would nor could make a book and tell lies all the time they were writing it, saying, *"Thus saith the Lord,"* when it was their own invention. It could not be the invention of bad men or devils, for they would not make a book that commands all duty, forbids all sin, and condemns their souls to hell for eternity.

Therefore, I draw this conclusion; the Bible must be given by divine inspiration.[15]

This unusual argument has influenced many people to believe!

In summary, some of many evidences for the Bible being the Word of God are:

1. Claims in the Bible
2. Christ's endorsement
3. Canonization of Scripture
4. Copying accuracy of Old Testament documents
5. Correlation of New Testament documents
6. Choice of biblical languages
7. Climatic conditions in Israel

---

15. Ibid., p. 123.

8. Complete unity of the Bible
9. Concise prophecies and their fulfillment
10. Capacity of the Bible to survive
11. Concise scientific data
12. Confirmation of historic data by archeology
13. Changeless truth
14. Capability to change lives
15. Common appeal and circulation of the Bible
16. Code of moral standards
17. The Church's success
18. Comforting and convicting power of the Bible
19. Conclusion of alternate appeal

Do you believe the Bible is God's infallible (incapable of error) and inerrant (without error) Word? If so, you have joined millions of others. The evidence is solid.

DISCUSSION QUESTIONS

IS THE BIBLE GOD'S WORD?

1. Which of the reasons given in this booklet to support the assertion the Bible is God's Word stands out to you as especially convincing?

2. Which reasons seem weak to you?

3. What reasons have you heard skeptics give for why they reject the Bible?

4. Do you think most believers and non-believers can adequately defend their own beliefs regarding the Bible's origin?

5. In your opinion, does it really matter whether or not the Bible is God's Word? Explain.

6. What is the Bible's view about its own origin? Give three supporting verses.

7. What evidence is found in the Bible to support the claim the New Testament is God's Word?

8. What view did the apostles Peter and Paul have regarding Scripture's author? Give verses to support your answer.

9. Did Jesus endorse the Bible as the Word of God? Give verses to support your answer.

10. Summarize each of the following evidences for why the Bible is the Word of God.

- Claims in the Bible

- Christ's endorsement

- Canonization of Scripture

- Copying accuracy of Old Testament documents

- Correlation of Old and New Testament documents

- Choice of biblical languages

- Climatic conditions in Israel

- Complete unity of the Bible

- Concise prophecies and their fulfillment

- Capacity of the Bible to survive

- Concise scientific data

- Confirmation of historic data by archeology

- Changeless truth

- Capability to change lives

- Common appeal and circulation of the Bible

- Code of moral standards

- The church's success

- Comforting and convicting power of the Bible

- Conclusion of alternate appeal

11. How has the information in this chapter affected your view of the Bible's authorship?

CHAPTER

THREE

WHO IS JESUS?

THE AVERAGE MAN ON THE STREET

Have you ever met someone who seemed to be the average person on the street, only to find out he or she was somewhat of a celebrity? It happened to me. My older brother was being recruited for college football, and one of the recruiters came to our high school and then to dinner at our home. He was polite and spent the evening asking us about ourselves, never really mentioning much about his own background. Because he was average size and didn't portray the rough-tumble football type, I concluded he probably had never played football himself.

The incident faded in my memory until a few years later when I discovered that the recruiter was Ken Hatfield: all-state athlete in two high school sports (one being football), college academic all-American, and leading punt returner in the nation his senior year at the University of Arkansas. This information came via the book

Courage To Conquer, which had stories of various well-known athletes. Since that time, Ken Hatfield has also been the head coach at such schools as the Air Force Academy, the University of Arkansas, and Clemson University.

Discovering these facts surprised me. It definitely was a case of misplaced identity. My preconceived notions and Ken's casual manner had caused me to draw a wrong conclusion. The old adage holds true, "You can't judge a book by its cover."

But what does misplaced identity have to do with Jesus? Many people see Him as the baby in the manger at Christmas who never became anything more than a meek and mild-mannered teacher. Others view Him as nothing more than a religious leader like Buddha or Mohammed. Still, others have only heard His name as a swear word. Indeed, Jesus has been the object of many misplaced identities.

The purpose of this study is to search out and discover Jesus' true identity. In doing so, the following questions will be asked and answered – What are Jesus' misplaced identities? What identity is supported by the evidence? With these thoughts in mind, let's begin.

WHAT ARE JESUS' MISPLACED IDENTITIES?

There was a time when Jesus asked His disciples (His followers) the question, *Who do people say that I am?"* He received several responses found in Matthew 16:13-16. Some said He was John the Baptist. Others said *Elijah, Jeremiah, or one of the prophets.* One disciple, Peter, said, *Thou art the Christ, the Son of the living God.*

In another passage, the Jewish authorities claimed that Jesus was demon-possessed. Matthew 12:22-24 records their accusation,

Then there was brought to Him (Jesus) a demon-possessed man who was blind and dumb, and He healed him, so that the dumb man spoke

and saw. And all the multitudes were amazed, and began to say, "This man cannot be the Son of David, can he?" But when the Pharisees heard it, they said, "This man casts out demons only by Beelzebul the ruler of the demons."

Just as confusion surrounded Jesus' identity in His day, much confusion still exists today. Regarding his identity, there are SEVEN basic options; six are misplaced, and a seventh is overwhelmingly supported by the evidence. Let's first examine the six.

1. Legend

The first misconception about Jesus' true identity is that He was a legend. The dictionary defines a legend as a story handed down from the past and not regarded as true history, although partly based on actual facts. Like King Arthur, Paul Bunyan, or other legendary figures, some people regard Jesus and the stories about Him as the result of someone's fertile imagination mixed with a pinch of reality.

Although this view makes sense to a few skeptics, it is rather uninformed. Even outside of the Bible, overwhelming evidence exists for Jesus' life and great works. The famous Jewish historian, Josephus, wrote about Jesus in his Antiquities of the Jews, "Now there was about this time Jesus a wise man, if it be lawful to call him a man; for he was a doer of wonderful works, a teacher of such men as receive the truth with pleasure. He drew over to him both many of the Jews and many of the Gentiles... And the tribe of Christians, so named for him, are not extinct at this day."[1]

Think of our Western calendar and the centrality of Christ. The key holidays, Christmas and Easter, are all about Him. Christmas honors Christ's birth, and Easter celebrates His resurrection. If Jesus

---

1. *Josephus, Antiquities of the Jews, (John C. Winston Company), 535.*

was the figment of someone's imagination, there is no way He could have become our calendar's central focus.

Even our calendar's dating system revolves around Jesus. The year AD 2002 means 2002 years since the birth of Christ. Some people think AD means After Death. Actually, it is two Latin words anno Domini meaning, "In the year of our Lord," dated from Christ's birth. BC means Before Christ. If AD meant After Death, the 33 years that Jesus walked the earth would be lost from the calendar. Having BC mean Before Christ, and AD mean in the year of our Lord (dated from His birth), no years are lost. Again, to think that a legendary figure could become the central figure upon which the Western calendar is based is a bit naïve.

As an interesting side note, in recent years there has been a very silent but deliberate attempt by those who oppose Christianity to remove anything Christian from society. One rather covert way is by changing the calendar dating system. Rather than BC meaning "Before Christ," writers have changed dates in new textbooks to read BCE, defined as "Before the Common Era". Unsuspecting readers and children in schools are caught totally unaware. Rather than having a calendar that for centuries revolved around Jesus, it now revolves around nothing. Ironically, however, even though BCE no longer includes the word "Christ," it still is based on the arrival of Jesus.

There is more historic evidence for Jesus' existence than for any other person in ancient times. The idea that Jesus is a legend is simply incorrect.

2. Learned Teacher or Prophet

Just as other religions have their great teachers, some people see Jesus as the learned (extremely knowledgeable) teacher or prophet of Christianity, but nothing more. This is not only a popular view today among non-Christians; it was popular during Jesus' time. When people addressed Jesus, they often called Him teacher. Matthew 8:19, 20 records such an incident, *And a certain scribe came and said to Him, "Teacher, I will follow You wherever You go." And Jesus said to him, "The foxes have holes, and the birds of the air have nests; but the Son of Man has nowhere to lay His head."*

In Matthew 9:11, the Pharisees referred to Jesus as a teacher, *And when the Pharisees saw this, they said to His disciples, "Why is your Teacher eating with the tax-gatherers and sinners?"*

Besides being a teacher, Jesus was also a prophet. He referred to Himself as such in Luke 13:33 when He talked about His upcoming death, *Nevertheless I must journey on today and tomorrow and the next day; for it cannot be that a prophet should perish outside of Jerusalem.*

Although Jesus was a great teacher who taught amazing truth, and a prophet who spoke prophetically, these are not adequate explanations of His total identity. The reason is, He also claimed to be God. John 10:30-33 records the incident and Jesus' own words,

> *"I and the Father are one." The Jews took up stones again to stone Him. Jesus answered them, "I showed you many good works from the Father; for which of them are you stoning Me?" The Jews answered Him, "For a good work we do not stone You, but for blasphemy; and because You, being a man, make Yourself out to be God."*

In this passage, Jesus said He and the Father are one. The Jews understood His claim and wanted to stone Him, believing He was only a man. If they were right, and Jesus' claim was false, at best, He was a lunatic or liar.

3. Lunatic

Because Jesus claimed to be God some people say He was crazed with delusions of grandeur. Although this view pleases some folks, Jesus' life did not fit the pattern of lunacy. He lived an emotionally stable life. His actions and interactions with people (except religious hypocrites) were loving and kind, even in the pain and agony of crucifixion. When others were out of control, Jesus remained rock-steady. Nothing in Jesus' life indicates He was crazy. This accusation is groundless.

4. Liar

Because Jesus claimed to be God some people accuse Him of lying in order to gain a following so He could set up a personal kingdom. Again, nothing in His life indicates He ever lied to anyone. On the contrary, he told the truth even when it was not to His benefit. One such account is found in Matthew 26:59-68 when He was on trial before the high priest.

> *Now the chief priests and the whole Council kept trying to obtain false testimony against Jesus, in order that they might put Him to death; and they did not find any, even though many false witnesses came forward. But later on, two came forward, and said, "This man stated, 'I am able to destroy the temple of God and to rebuild it in three days.'" And the high priest stood up and said to Him, "Do You make no answer? What is it that these men are testifying against You?" But Jesus kept silent. And the high priest said to Him, "I adjure You by the living God, that You tell us whether You are the Christ, the Son of God." Jesus said to him, "You have said it yourself nevertheless I tell you, hereafter you shall see the Son of Man sitting at the right hand of Power and coming on the clouds of heaven." Then the high priest tore his*

robes, saying, "He has blasphemed! What further need do we have of witnesses? Behold, you have now heard the blasphemy; what do you think? "They answered and said," He is deserving of death! "Then they spat in His face and beat Him with their fists; and others slapped Him, and said, "Prophesy to us, you Christ; who is the one who hit you?"

Jesus never tried to set up His own earthly kingdom but always talked about His Father's kingdom and how He had to die and rise from the dead to give people the opportunity to enter that kingdom. The claim that Christ was a liar has no factual support.

5. Lucifer's Emissary

In Jesus' time, there were those who believed that Jesus was an agent of Satan. In Matthew 12:24, the Pharisees accused Him of casting out demons by using Satanic power. Jesus' response was quite clear,

Any kingdom divided against itself is laid waste; and any city or house divided against itself shall not stand. And if Satan casts out Satan, he is divided against himself; how then shall his kingdom stand? (Matthew 12:25,26)

In other words, if Jesus worked for Satan, it would make no sense for Him to cast out demons. He would be working against His own boss! The fact is, Jesus worked for God the Father and cast out demons on many occasions (Matthew 8:28-34, Luke 4:33-35, Luke 4:41).

The notion that Jesus worked for Satan was and is irrational. At every turn, Jesus opposed Satan. He certainly was not Lucifer's emissary!

6. Lesser God

Since Jesus was not a legend, lunatic, liar, or Lucifer's emissary, and since He was more than a learned teacher/prophet, what options are left regarding His true identity? Actually, there are only two. The first is that He was some type of deity but not equal with God, the creator of the universe. This view is held today by nearly every cult. They say Jesus was and is God's Son but not equal with God the Father. They say He is a *lesser God*. To support their view cults say the Bible teaches there are other gods.

Indeed, the Bible does teach there are many gods (with a little g). The judges of Israel are referred to as gods in Psalm 58:1-3 and again in Psalm 82:6. This did not mean they were deities like God but instead that they sat in positions of power, administering God's justice on the earth. They acted as God's representatives.

In the Old Testament, the children of Israel fashioned a god of gold. Exodus 32:3-4 states

> *Then all the people tore off the gold rings which were in their ears and brought them to Aaron. And he took this from their hand, and fashioned it with a graving tool, and made it into a molten calf; and they said, "This is your god, O Israel, who brought you up from the land of Egypt."*

In addition, the pagan peoples of the Bible worshiped gods of their own making, but all of these gods, including the molten calf, were really just idols. They had no real power or authority and could not help or hurt anyone. That is why the one true God gave the Israelites the Ten Commandments. The first commandment instructed the people not to worship anything or anyone but the one true God. Exodus 20:1-6 states,

Then God spoke all these words, saying, "I am the LORD your God, who brought you out of the land of Egypt, out of the house of slavery. You shall have no other gods before Me. You shall not make for yourself an idol, or any likeness of what is in heaven above or on the earth beneath or in the water under the earth. You shall not worship them or serve them; for I, the LORD your God, am a jealous God, visiting the iniquity of the fathers on the children, on the third and the fourth generations of those who hate Me, but showing lovingkindness to thousands, to those who love Me and keep My commandments."

1 Corinthians 8:5-6 sheds more light on this subject:

For even if there are so-called gods whether in heaven or on earth, as indeed there are many gods and many lords, yet for us there is but one God, the Father, from whom are all things, and we exist for Him; and one Lord, Jesus Christ, by whom are all things, and we exist through Him.

In Jesus' time, the Greeks and Romans had innumerable false gods and lords. The same is true today. Even though most people in modern times don't bow down to idols, they have made their work, their hobbies, their recreation, or something else their gods. Their false gods are the things that command their devotion and consume their time.

No matter what gods or lords people have in their lives, there is still only one true God and Lord. That one God is in three persons: God the Father, God the Son (Jesus), and God the Holy Spirit. These three comprise the one triune Godhead called the Trinity. The Trinity will be looked at in more depth in future pages.

The view that Jesus is a lesser God does not square with other passages of Scripture, either. Isaiah 43:10,11 makes it clear there is only one God, and will never be any others.

> *"You are My witnesses," declares the Lord, "And My servant whom I have chosen, in order that you may know and believe Me, and understand that I am He. Before Me there was no God formed, and there will be none after Me. I, even I, am the Lord; and there is no savior besides Me."*

To say Jesus is a lesser God would mean there is more than one God, but the above verses do not leave this option open. In the passage, God the Father clearly states there is only one God. There were no Gods formed either before or after Him! Therefore, Jesus can't be some lesser God.

If Jesus is not a legend, lunatic, liar, Lucifer's emissary, or a lesser God, and if He is more than a learned teacher and prophet, who is he? This brings us to the second major question to be answered, "What identity is supported by the evidence?"

WHAT IS JESUS' TRUE IDENTITY?

The only option left for Jesus' identity is that He was and is the LORD, God in human flesh! How do we know this? First, He performed amazing miracles that were witnessed by many people. He healed the sick, gave sight to the blind, read people's minds, walked on water, calmed a storm, multiplied food, turned water into wine, and even raised the dead. Only God could do these things.

Illusionists and tricksters can do many amazing feats through sleight of hand, but Jesus' miracles were beyond the realm of illusion. They were true miracles. For example, no one but God could walk on water in the midst of a storm in the middle of an unfrozen lake. No one but God could raise someone who had been dead for several days.

Even beyond His miracles, the testimony in the Bible overwhelming points to the fact that Jesus is none other than God Himself.

SEVEN MORE REASONS WHY JESUS IS LORD

1. Jesus Claimed Equality with God

As stated previously, in John 10:30-33, Jesus claimed to be equal with God the Father,

> Jesus said, *"I and the Father are one." The Jews took up stones again to stone Him. Jesus answered them, "I showed you many good works from the Father; for which of them are you stoning Me?" The Jews answered Him, "For a good work we do not stone You, but for blasphemy; and because You, being a man, make Yourself out to be God."*

When Jesus said, *"I and the Father are one,"* He was not saying He was the same person as the Father, for they are different persons in the Godhead or Trinity (Father, Son, and Holy Spirit). He was saying He had the same essence, nature, and power as God the Father. The Jews understood exactly what He meant. He was claiming equality with God. That's why they wanted to kill Him.

Why did Jesus claim equality with God? He claimed it because it was true! The fact that Jesus claimed to be God does not prove He is, but it certainly makes His feelings about His identity crystal clear!

2. Jesus is Called the Word, and the Word is Equal with God

John 1:1 states, *"In the beginning was the Word, and the Word was with God, and the Word was God."*

Listen now to John 1:14, a little later on in the passage, *"And the Word became flesh, and dwelt among us, and we beheld His glory, glory as of the only begotten from the Father, full of grace and truth."*

In these two verses, the Bible not only makes it clear *the Word* was *with God,* but *the Word was* God. It also makes it clear *the Word became flesh and dwelt among us.* Who became flesh by coming from heaven to be born a baby and dwell among us? Jesus! Who was and is *the Word?* JESUS!

If the WORD is God, and the WORD is also Jesus, then Jesus is God. When two entities are equal to a third entity, they are equal to each other.

3. Jesus Forgives Sin

The Bible testifies that Jesus is God because He has the authority to forgive sins, and this authority is God's alone. Listen to Luke 5:20, 21, *And seeing their faith, He (Jesus) said, "Friend, your sins are forgiven you." And the scribes and the Pharisees began to reason, saying, "Who is this man who speaks blasphemies? Who can forgive sins, but God alone?"*

The Jewish religious leaders knew only God had the authority to forgive sins. When Jesus claimed He had this authority, they accused Him of blasphemy. They failed to see Who He was and is.

Since God alone has the authority to forgive sins, yet Jesus forgives sins, then Jesus must be God.

4. Jesus is the One Who Created All Things

Did you know that Jesus created all things? It's true. This is one more reason He is God. Genesis 1:1 states, *In the beginning, God created the heavens and the earth.* According to Scripture, there is no doubt that God is the Creator of all things. Yet John 1:1-3 clearly states the Word (Jesus) created everything,

In the beginning was the Word, and the Word was with God, and the Word was God. He was in the beginning with God. All things came into being by Him (Jesus, the Word), *and apart from Him nothing came into being that has come into being.*

Colossians 1:16, 17 also refers to Jesus as the Creator,

For by Him (Jesus) all things were created both in the heavens and on earth, visible and invisible, whether thrones or dominions or rulers or authorities – all things have been created by Him and for Him. And He is before all things, and in Him all things hold together.

These verses make it clear that Jesus is the Creator. If God is the Creator, and yet Jesus is the Creator, then Jesus is God.

5. Jesus is to be Worshiped

The fifth reason why Jesus is God is because He is worthy of worship. Exodus 20:1-5 makes it clear that God alone is to be worshiped,

Then God spoke all these words, saying, "I am the LORD your God, who brought you out of the land of Egypt, out of the house of slavery. You shall have no other gods before Me. You shall not make for yourself an idol, or any likeness of what is in heaven above or on the earth beneath or in the water under the earth. You shall not worship them or serve them; for I, the LORD your God, am a jealous God, visiting the iniquity of the fathers on the children, on the third and the fourth generations of those who hate Me."

God's people are to have no other gods or worship any. On the other hand, the following verses clearly teach that Jesus is to be worshiped. In Hebrews 1:5,6, angels are instructed to worship Jesus,

For to which of the angels did He ever say, "Thou art My Son, today I have begotten Thee"? And again, "I will be a Father to Him and He shall be a Son to Me"? And when He again brings the first-born into the world, He says, "And let all the angels of God worship Him."

Philippians 2:10,11 says all people will worship Jesus:

"That at the name of Jesus every knee should bow, of those who are in heaven, and on earth, and under the earth, and that every tongue should confess that Jesus Christ is Lord, to the glory of God the Father."

In Revelation 7:9-11 Jesus is worshiped in heaven:

After these things I looked, and behold, a great multitude, which no one could count, from every nation and all tribes and peoples and tongues, standing before the throne and before the Lamb (Jesus), clothed in white robes, and palm branches were in their hands; and they cry out with a loud voice, saying, "Salvation to our God who sits on the throne, and to the Lamb." And all the angels were standing around the throne and around the elders and the four living creatures; and they fell on their faces before the throne and worshiped God.

Notice in the above passage that God the Father and the Son (the Lamb) are both worshiped by angels. In the last verse they are both simply referred to together as God.

69

If only God is to be worshiped, and yet Jesus is to be worshiped, then Jesus must be God.

6. Thomas' Testimony Confirms Jesus is God

When Jesus rose from the dead and first showed Himself alive to a group of His disciples, Thomas was not present. Upon hearing the news, Thomas refused to believe. In John 20:25, Thomas stated, *Unless I see in His hands the imprint of the nails, and put my finger into the place of the nails, and put my hand into His side, I will not believe.* Soon afterwards Jesus appeared again. This time, Thomas was present. Seeing Jesus alive changed Thomas' mind and caused him to make an amazing declaration recorded in John 20:26-29. Listen to the account,

> *And after eight days again His disciples were inside, and Thomas with them. Jesus came, the doors having been shut, and stood in their midst, and said, "Peace be with you." Then He said to Thomas, "Reach here your finger, and see My hands; and reach here your hand, and put it into My side; and be not unbelieving but believing." Thomas answered and said to Him, "My Lord and my God!" Jesus said to Him, "Because you have seen Me, have you believed? Blessed are they who did not see, and yet believed."*

When Thomas saw Jesus alive, he declared, *My Lord and My God!* If Jesus was not Lord and God, He would have corrected Thomas and set the record straight. He did not, but instead told Thomas that the truly blessed ones were those, like Christians today, who having not seen Jesus in the flesh, but still believe.

Thomas' declaration is another indication from Scripture that Jesus is God.

· · ·

7. The Trinity

One more indication that Jesus is God is the doctrine of the Trinity. Simply stated, the Bible teaches that there is only one God, but that three beings are called God. Those three (Father, Son, and Holy Spirit) make up the one God. Listen again to the words of Isaiah 43:10,11,

> *"You are My witnesses," declares the Lord, "And My servant whom I have chosen, in order that you may know and believe Me, and understand that I am He. Before Me there was no God formed, and there will be none after Me. I, even I, am the Lord."*

This passage clearly teaches there is only one God. There were no "Gods" formed before the one true God, nor will there be any after Him. This does not insinuate that God Himself was formed, for He is eternal. It simply means that there are no other Gods besides Him, period!

Yet, three persons are called God. God the Father is obviously called God. We have already seen that God the Son (Jesus) is called God. And in Acts 5:1-4, the Holy Spirit is also called God. Listen carefully to the passage.

> *But a certain man named Ananias, with his wife Sapphira, sold a piece of property, and kept back some of the price for himself, with his wife's full knowledge, and bringing a portion of it, he laid it at the apostles' feet. But Peter said, "Ananias, why has Satan filled your heart to lie to the Holy Spirit, and to keep back some of the price of the land? While it remained unsold, did it not remain your own? And after it was sold, was it not under your control? Why is it that you have conceived this deed in your heart? You have not lied to men, but to God."*

Ananias and Sapphira were not obligated to sell their piece of property or to give all of the proceeds to the church. It was a choice they made freely. The problem arose when they lied about it. They said they gave the entire amount when, in fact, they kept back some for themselves. If they had said they were giving a lesser portion, that would have been fine. If they had not wanted to give any, this, too, would have been acceptable. The problem was they said they gave it all but did not.

This passage makes it clear that by lying to the Holy Spirit, the couple lied to God. People don't lie to a force; they lie to another person. In this case, that other person was none other than the Holy Spirit, the third person in the Godhead or Trinity.

There is one passage where all three (Father, Son, and Holy Spirit) are mentioned together. Matthew 28:19 records some of Jesus' parting words to His disciples, *"Go therefore and make disciples of all the nations, baptizing them in the name of the FATHER and THE SON and THE HOLY SPIRIT..."*

Notice that Jesus says in the *name*, not in the *names* of the Father, Son and Holy Spirit. Why? Because Father, Son, and Holy Spirit are one God. Collectively, they are the Godhead! They have a single name: God!

Even though the idea of three in one is difficult for the human mind to grasp, God has placed trinities all around us to help us better understand His nature. For example, time is made up of past, present, and future time, yet it is all one continuum of time. We live in a universe of time, space, and matter, yet it is a single universe. Water can be liquid, steam, or ice and, yet it is all one molecular substance, H_2O. To measure the location of something in a room, the three dimensions of length, width, and depth are needed, yet they give a single location. An egg has a shell, an egg white, and a yoke, yet it is one egg.

In relation to God, it is not that God changes from one form to another (from Father to Son to Spirit and back again). This would be modalism. Instead, He is three in one at the same time. This may be hard to grasp in our finite minds, but it must be remembered that God is infinite!

ARE THERE PASSAGES THAT SEEM TO INDICATE JESUS ISN'T GOD?

There are a few passages that some people try to use to show Jesus is inferior to God, but, when understood in the proper context, these verses do not contradict the clear teaching that Jesus is God.

John 14:28

In John 14:28, Jesus states, *You heard that I said to you, "I go away, and I will come to you." If you loved Me, you would have rejoiced, because I go to the Father; for the Father is greater than I.* In this verse, Jesus announced to His disciples that He would soon leave earth and return to the Father, who was greater than He. Does this verse teach that Jesus is inferior to the Father, making Him a lesser God? Absolutely not!

It must be remembered that Jesus is not only God, He was also a man. He was the God-man – God in human flesh. Although fully human (He had a human body), He was also fully God (He possessed all the fullness of the Godhead). John 14:28 simply refers to the fact that the physical part of Jesus was inferior to the Father who was pure Spirit. But on the flip side, Jesus' spiritual nature was equal with God the Father. That's why He said in John 10:30, *I and the Father are one.*

In Colossians 2:9 the apostle Paul confirmed the fact that all the fullness of Deity was in Christ even in His earthly body, *For in Him all the fullness of Deity dwells in bodily form.*

John 10:31-33 also makes the point of Jesus' Deity crystal-clear,

The Jews took up stones again to stone Him. Jesus answered them, "I showed you many good works from the Father; for which of them are you stoning Me?" The Jews answered Him, "For a good work we do not stone You, but for blasphemy; and because You, being a man, make Yourself out to be God."

Jesus was not just claiming *to be like* God. He was claiming *to be* God. The Jews understood exactly what He was saying and wanted to kill Him for it.

Philippians 2:5-7

Another set of verses some people use to try to disprove Jesus' divinity is Philippians 2:5-7. The passage states,

Have this attitude in yourselves which was also in Christ Jesus, who, although He existed in the form of God, did not regard equality with God a thing to be grasped, but emptied Himself, taking the form of a bondservant, and being made in the likeness of men.

Some skeptics say this verse teaches that Jesus did not try to be equal with God, but was really something less. Again, this is an incorrect interpretation.

Notice the verse says, *Although He (Jesus) existed in the form of God, He did not regard equality with God a thing to be grasped.* The word *form* refers to essential form. In other words, Jesus had the essential form of God and was equal to God the Father from eternity past. When He came to earth and took on human flesh in order to die for our sins, He emptied Himself. This emptying does not mean

He lost His divine attributes, but that He merely laid them aside and chose not to use them at certain times. For example, when Jesus traveled, He could have transported Himself instantaneously from one place to another, but instead chose to walk. He could have made it so He didn't need sleep or food, but instead chose to rest and eat. He even allowed Himself to feel the pain of crucifixion.

On the flip side, there were many times when He did use His divine attributes, like when He walked on water, healed the sick, and raised the dead. Jesus' emptying did not undo His Deity; it was really a confirmation of it.

The next verses in Philippians further confirm that Jesus laid aside His divine attributes in order to die for the sins of mankind,

And being found in appearance as a man, He humbled Himself by becoming obedient to the point of death, even death on a cross. Therefore also God (the Father) highly exalted Him, and bestowed on Him the name which is above every name, that at the name of Jesus every knee should bow, of those who are in heaven, and on earth, and under the earth, and that every tongue should confess that Jesus Christ is Lord, to the glory of God the Father (Philippians 2:8-11).

The Son glorified the Father, and the Father honored the Son. Indeed, Jesus Christ is Lord. He is the King of kings and the Lord of lords.

Colossians 1:15-17

Another passage that is often used to try to disprove Christ's equality with God is Colossians 1:15-17,

And He (Jesus) is the image of the invisible God, the firstborn of all creation. For by Him all things were created, both in the heavens and on earth, visible and invisible, whether thrones or dominions or rulers or authorities – all things have been created by Him and for Him. And He is before all things, and in Him all things hold together.

The argument against Christ's Deity goes as follows: as God's Son, Jesus was the firstborn. If He was born, then He didn't live forever. If He didn't live forever, then He can't be God because one of God's primary attributes is that He is eternal.

To properly understand these verses, it is vital to understand the term firstborn. Although the term firstborn can mean the first one born, it is also a term used to designate position and authority. In the context of Colossians 1:15-17, the latter is the correct rendering. It is not that Jesus was created by the Father for then there would be a second God created, and we have already seen in Isaiah 43:10,11 that there were no Gods created before or after God. Again, those verses state,

"You are My witnesses," declares the Lord, "And My servant whom I have chosen, in order that you may know and believe Me, and understand that I am He. Before Me there was no God formed, and there will be none after Me. I, even I, am the Lord."

The term firstborn, when used of Jesus, speaks of His position and authority over all creation because He made it. Just as a firstborn son in the Old Testament was given the position of prominence in the family whereby he inherited the greatest amount, so too, Jesus holds the position of firstborn and has authority over the whole universe.

In another sense, it is true that Jesus was God's firstborn in that

He left His place in heaven with the Father and the Holy Spirit and was born as a human in order to become 'Immanuel' which means 'God with us.' Matthew 1:23-25 makes this point clear,

Behold, the virgin shall be with child, and shall bear a Son, and they shall call His name Immanuel, which translated means, God with us. And Joseph arose from his sleep and did as the angel of the Lord commanded him, and took her as his wife, and kept her a virgin until she gave birth to a Son; and he called His name Jesus.

It is true that Jesus was born in His humanity. John 1:14 states, *And the Word (Jesus) became flesh, and dwelt among us, and we saw His glory, glory as of the only begotten from the Father, full of grace and truth.* But in His Deity, Jesus existed from eternity past. That's why John 1:1-3 states,

In the beginning was the Word, and the Word was with God, and the Word was God. He was in the beginning with God. All things came into being by Him, and apart from Him nothing came into being that has come into being.

Jesus was already with the Father in the beginning. He preexisted the creation. That's why the verses state, *apart from Him nothing came into being that has come into being.* If Jesus was a created being, this passage would mean that He would have had to create Himself since nothing came into being apart from Him. This is a logical impossibility. He didn't create Himself; He already existed. That's why He responded to the Jews the way He did in John 8:57-59,

The Jews therefore said to Him, "You are not yet fifty years old, and have You seen Abraham?" Jesus said to them, "Truly, truly, I say to you, before Abraham was born, I am." Therefore they picked up stones to throw at Him; but Jesus hid Himself, and went out of the temple.

By Jesus saying, *before Abraham was born, I am,* He was confirming His pre-existence. He was declaring He was God and had existed from eternity past. No wonder the Jews tried to stone Him! They thought He was speaking blasphemy!

1 Corinthians 11:3

Some people try to use 1 Corinthians 11:3 to show that Jesus is inferior to God. In this verse, Paul states, *But I want you to understand that Christ is the head of every man, and the man is the head of a woman, and God is the head of Christ.*

The question arises, "If God is the head of Christ, doesn't that make Jesus inferior to God? The answer is no! If this argument were true, it would also mean that women are inferior to men because the verse also states, *The man is the head of a woman.* Women are not inferior to men; they simply have a different role to fulfill in God's economy. Galatians 3:28 makes it clear that men and women are equal in God's sight *There is neither Jew nor Greek, there is neither slave nor free man, there is neither male nor female; for you are all one in Christ Jesus.*

Although women are to submit to their husbands in marriage (Ephesians 5:22) and not to usurp men's authority (1 Timothy 2:12), these are not statements of inferiority but indicators of chain of command. The Godhead also has a chain of command. Although Father, Son, and Holy Spirit are co-equal and co-eternal, the Son willingly submits to the Father. That is why Jesus said in the garden of Gethsemane, *not as I will, but as you will* (Matthew 26:39). That is also why Jesus willingly left His throne in heaven to come to earth to be born as a baby in a manger and eventually die for the sin of mankind (Philippians 2:6-8).

This point is further illustrated in the military. I was stationed at an Air Force Base where the Base Commander and the Wing Commander were both colonels. At the staff meeting, the Base Commander called the Wing Commander, "Sir." As a young officer, I wondered why one colonel called another, "Sir," then I realized that although they were equal in rank, the Wing Commander was higher in the chain of command.

Matthew 26:39

Yet another verse used by some to try to show that Jesus is inferior to the Father is Matthew 26:39. This verse records Jesus' prayer to the Father in the garden of Gethsemane shortly before Jesus was arrested, tried, and crucified. The verse states, *And He (Jesus) went a little beyond them (the disciples), and fell on His face and prayed, saying, "My Father, if it is possible, let this cup pass from Me; yet not as I will, but as you wilt."*

In these verses, Jesus prayed to the Father. If Jesus is God, isn't it illogical that He would pray to Himself? In this regard, it must be remembered that although the Godhead (Father, Son, and Holy Spirit) are One, they are also individual persons. It is thus not illogical to think of Jesus in his humanity praying to the Father.

WHO IS JESUS?

The Bible not only teaches that Jesus is God, it also clearly shows He is part of a Trinity composed of Father, Son, and Holy Spirit.

So, WHO is JESUS? He is not a LEGEND. He is much more than a

LEARNED TEACHER OR PROPHET. He is not a LUNATIC. He is not a LIAR. He is not LUCIFER'S EMISSARY. He is not a LESSER god. He is LORD!

This fact is confirmed by the myriads of miracles Jesus performed and by the Scriptures' testimony.

Since Jesus is Lord, the question arises, "How should people respond to Him?" This will be the subject of chapter 8, "How does a person get into heaven?"

DISCUSSION QUESTIONS

WHO IS JESUS?

1. Now or in the past, what has been your position on the true identity of Jesus? Why?

2. Is there any part of this chapter that stands out in your mind as helpful? Explain.

3. What is a legend? Why is this possibility a poor choice for the true identity of Jesus? How does our modern calendar apply?

4. Even though Jesus was a teacher and a prophet, why are these inadequate descriptions of His true identity? How does John 10:30-33 apply?

5. Why do some people accuse Jesus of being a lunatic or liar? Why do these identities not fit Him?

6. Read Matthew 12:24-26. What accusation did the religious leaders make regarding Jesus' identity, and what was Jesus' reply?

7. Some people say that Jesus is a lesser god, but not the true God. What light does Isaiah 43:10,11 shed on the subject?

8. Do you think Jesus' miracles are strong evidence He is God? Why or why not?

9. What are the different reasons given in this booklet to support the view that Jesus is God? Briefly summarize each one.

10. What verses in the Bible do some people use to try to show that Jesus is not God? Briefly explain why each argument is false.

FOUR

IS THE RESURRECTION TRUE?

On Easter, Christians around the world celebrate Jesus' resurrection, claiming He rose from the dead nearly 2,000 years ago. But isn't it a little far-fetched to believe that anyone could rise from the dead? A true resurrection would go against the laws of nature.

Even today, with the best modern medicine and technology, no one rises from the dead. It is true that doctors can restart a person's heart after it has stopped for a few minutes, but no one can revive someone who has been dead for three days. That would be a miracle!

Have you ever asked the question, "Is there any solid evidence for the resurrection, or does a person simply need to believe it on blind faith?" Many people have never asked this question, but they should. And the good news is – there is solid evidence the resurrection really happened.

If you are a Christian and don't know the evidence, the following information will encourage you and increase your faith. If you are not a Christian, the evidence may show you your need to investigate further Jesus' claims.

THE RELEVANCE OF THE RESURRECTION

Is the resurrection really that important? Absolutely! It is the crux of Christianity! To put it bluntly, the resurrection is the single issue upon which Christianity rises or falls. Paul the apostle understood this point and wrote in 1 Corinthians 15:14, *"And if Christ has not been raised, then our preaching is vain, your faith also is vain."*

Why did Paul say Christian faith is vain unless the resurrection is true? He knew if Jesus did not rise from the dead, He was nothing more than a man. As a mere man, He could not guarantee eternal life to anyone. If He was only a man and yet made the outrageous claim to be equal with God, He must have been a liar, lunatic, or something worse. If so, Christianity is false, and the Bible can be considered interesting reading but not the inspired Word of God.

If Christ did not rise from the dead, millions of people have been deceived into believing one of the greatest hoaxes of all time. On the other hand, if Christ did rise, He conquered the one thing – death – that has baffled and grieved humankind through the ages. In conquering death, Christ validated His claim as God and proved Christianity to be true.

The Bible teaches that when people die, they eventually either go to heaven or hell. Jesus claimed to be the ONLY way to heaven (John 14:6). If you reject Him, and it turns out that what He said about Himself is false, you have lost NOTHING! On the other hand, if you reject Him, and what He said is true, you have lost EVERYTHING!

It has been said that of all world religions, the four largest are based on the personalities of men rather than philosophic ideas. All of these men died and have remained dead except one – Jesus!

Abraham, the father of Judaism, died in 1900 BC. The exact date of Buddha's death is unknown, but the earliest accounts say that when he died, it was with an utter passing away, and nothing was left behind. Mohammed, the founder of Islam, died June 8, AD 632, at age 61 in Medina, where his tomb is visited annually by countless Muslims. Jesus died and was buried, but His followers believe He rose from the dead on the third day after His death.

Only Christians worship a risen Savior, Jesus! Only Christianity is based on the supernatural event of someone conquering death. This is what sets it apart. Skeptics know the critical nature of the resurrection. They realize that if Jesus conquered death, His claim to be God must be true. That is why they have tried so hard to disprove the resurrection. So far, no one has succeeded, and many have put their faith in Christ in the process.

It is no surprise that God chose the resurrection to put His stamp of approval on Christianity. Since death has baffled man from the beginning of time, a true resurrection would be a clear indication of God's hand at work.

Is the resurrection relevant to the Christian faith? Without a doubt! The question then arises, "Is there any real evidence to support a true resurrection?" Again, the answer is a resounding yes!

For a more in-depth study of the following reasons why the resurrection is true, I highly recommend the best-selling books Evidence that Demands A Verdict and More Evidence that Demands A Verdict by Josh McDowell. It is interesting to note that McDowell was one of those skeptics who set out to disprove the resurrection and became a Christian in the process. There are other men like Lee Strobel who have also come to Christ after trying to disprove Christianity. His book, *The Case for Christ*, and his other books are extremely well done and give solid evidence for the validity of Christianity.

EVIDENCE FOR THE RESURRECTION

1. Christ's Own Claims

The first evidence for the resurrection involves the claims of Christ. He predicted He would rise.

Matthew 12:38-4 states:

Then some of the scribes and Pharisees answered Him [Jesus], saying, "Teacher, we want to see a sign from You." But He answered and said to them, "An evil and adulterous generation craves for a sign; and yet no sign shall be given to it but the sign of Jonah the prophet; for just as Jonah was three days and three nights in the belly of the sea monster, so shall the Son of Man be three days and three nights in the heart of the earth."

Matthew 16:21 states:

From that time Jesus Christ began to show His disciples that He must go to Jerusalem, and suffer many things from the elders and chief priests and scribes, and be killed, and be raised up on the third day.

Matthew 17:9 states:

And as they were coming down from the mountain, Jesus commanded them saying, "Tell the vision to no one until the Son of Man has risen from the dead."

Matthew 17:22,23 states:

And while they were gathering together in Galilee, Jesus said to them, "The Son of Man is going to be delivered into the hands of men; and they will kill Him, and He will be raised again on the third day." And they were deeply grieved.

Although Jesus referred to Himself at times as "The Son of Man," He also referred to Himself as "The Son of God" (John 3:16). He was both. He was "The Son of Man" in the sense that He took on bodily form on earth. He was "The Son of God" as part of the Trinity (Father, Son, and Holy Spirit). He was the God-man.

It is no big thing to predict you will die. Hebrews 9:27 says we will all die. A person can even predict how he will die. But for a person to predict his own death and subsequent resurrection in a specific number of days and then fulfill that prediction is beyond the realm of human possibility. Only God could perform such a miracle.

The followers of the great magician, Houdini, believe that someday he will come back from the dead – unfortunately, they will continue to be disappointed. On the other hand, Jesus predicted He would rise in three days, and He did.

2. History's Testimony

There is much evidence from history to support Christ's resurrection. One of the clearest evidences comes from the Jewish historian Josephus, who lived and wrote in the first century AD. Listen to his words taken from the "Antiquities of The Jews," page 535. This book records much of the history of the Jewish people.

Now there was about this time Jesus, a wise man if it be lawful to call him a man; for he was a doer of wonderful works, a teacher of such men as receive the truth with pleasure. He drew over to him both many of the Jews and many of the Gentiles. He was the Christ. And when Pilate, at the suggestion of the principal men amongst us, had condemned him to the cross, those that loved him at the first did not forsake him; for he appeared to them alive again the third day; as the divine prophets had foretold these and ten thousand other wonderful things concerning him. And the tribe of Christians, so named for him, are not extinct at this day.

As a Jewish historian, Josephus was much like a newsman reporting the facts. He also was primarily writing to please the Jews and the Romans who ruled his country. The only reason he would write that Jesus was the Christ was because he was absolutely convinced of the fact. As such, he was willing to risk his reputation and position to say so.

3. The Fact that Jesus was Dead

The third reason that the resurrection is true is because Jesus was dead. In order to have a true resurrection, the person who rises must have been dead. Although this seems obvious, some skeptics have postulated that Jesus never died. Instead, they say He only appeared to be dead and was mistakenly buried. In the coolness of the tomb, He revived and came out, appearing to conquer death. This is known as the Swoon Theory. Unfortunately for the skeptics, the facts do not support such a theory. The following gives clear evidence of why Jesus was DEAD.

Jesus was up most of the night and the whole morning before He was crucified (Matthew 26:36-27:32, Mark 14:22-15:21, Luke 22:39-23:25, John 18:1-19:15). Part of this time was spent agonizing in prayer in the Garden of Gethsemane over whether or not to go through with the crucifixion. The human part of Christ said, "No, I really don't want to do this!" The divine part said, "Yes, I need to do this in order to make a way for men to be saved!" Matthew 26:39, 42 records Christ's struggle and final decision, *My Father, if it is possible, let this cup pass from Me; yet not as I will, but as Thou wilt... My Father, if this cannot pass away unless I drink it, Your will be done.*

After His prayer vigil, Jesus was arrested and taken before the High Priest and the Sanhedrin, where He was falsely accused. He was later sent to the Governor, Pontius Pilate, then to King Herod, and finally back to Pilate. These activities undoubtedly kept Jesus up the rest of the night and through the next day before He was crucified. On the basis of sleep deprivation alone, Jesus was extremely tired.

Jesus was beaten and scourged (Matthew 26:67, Matthew 27:29,30, John 19:1).

On at least two occasions during the night and morning, Jesus' captors beat, slapped, and spit on Him. He was also scourged. Under Hebrew law, scourging entailed 40 lashes with a multi-stranded leather whip with sharp or blunt objects attached to each strand. Under Roman law, there was no limit to the number of lashes a person might receive. In Jesus' case, it is speculated that He probably received more than 40 lashes because the Romans administered the beating. Scourging left a victim's flesh and veins lacerated to the bone and often exposed internal organs.

At one point after Christ's scourging, the Roman soldiers put a mock royal robe on Him and beat and spat on Him. During this time, the cloth undoubtedly stuck to Jesus' bloodied back. He lost even more blood when they took this robe off and gave Him His own. Jesus was now getting closer to death.

Jesus was made to carry His own cross (John 19:16,17).

By the time Jesus was led away to be crucified, He was undoubtedly extremely weak. Although they initially forced Him to carry His own cross, it was clear that He could not carry it far (Mark 15:20,21). Roman soldiers then pressed Simon of Cyrene into service to carry it for Him. Also, the language used to describe Christ going

90

to the cross indicates He was so weak that He almost needed to be dragged or carried along.

Jesus went through a brutal crucifixion (Mark 15:24, Luke 23:33).

Crucifixion was a very painful and cruel way to die. The victim was made to lie face up on a wooden cross while large spikes were driven through his wrists and feet. The cross was then stood upright, and the base dropped in a hole, causing the flesh to rip and tear. Sometimes, victims hung on the cross for hours before they died. They usually did not die from loss of blood but from suffocation. The weight of their bodies caused their chest cavities to collapse. Even in great pain, they pushed up with their legs to get a breath. Eventually, soldiers broke their legs using clubs, making it impossible to push up. Suffocation followed.

Jesus had a spear thrust into His side (John 19:31-34).

When the Roman soldiers came to break Jesus' legs, He was already dead. His seemingly early death is quite understandable, considering He had not slept, had been beaten, scourged, made to carry his own cross, and hung on a cross. Instead of breaking his legs, the soldiers administered what was known as "The Death Stroke." They took a spear and jabbed it under Jesus' ribs into His heart. This ensured the death process was complete. As further indication that Jesus had already died, blood and water came out of his wound. The death stroke did not kill Christ; He was already dead. In addition, Roman law required that a death certificate be made for each victim. Before this could be completed, trained people had to declare that the victims were indeed dead. The swoon theory that Jesus didn't really die has no support and simply comes from someone's fertile imagination. Jesus was dead!

. . .

4. The Burial (John 19:38-42)

Jesus was buried in the tradition of the Jews. As a secret disciple of Christ, Joseph of Arimathea feared the Jews. Probably from a guilty conscience, he finally stepped forward and asked permission to give Jesus a decent burial. Nicodemus, another of Jesus' secret disciples, also came, bringing a vast quantity of myrrh and aloes for the burial process. When Jesus was taken from the cross, He was wrapped in linen cloth with the burial spices.

Myrrh was a gummy substance, and aloes resembled a crushed powdery substance like sawdust. The sweet-smelling mixture helped preserve the mummified body and reduced the stench. If Jesus was not dead when He was taken from the cross, He would have suffocated from being wrapped in these substances and laid in a tomb. In addition, there is no way (apart from Him being Deity) that Jesus could have physically gotten out of these wrappings by Himself. This further refutes the swoon theory.

5. The Guard (Matthew 27:62-66)

The fifth evidence for the resurrection relates to the guards around Jesus' tomb. After Jesus was buried, the Jewish leaders went to Pilate and asked that guards be placed around His tomb. They remembered His claim of rising from the dead on the third day. Apparently, the leaders feared that Jesus' followers would steal the body and bring a great deception upon the people. Pilate, therefore, authorized a group of Roman soldiers to secure the tomb.

On the day of Jesus' resurrection, the Bible says an angel rolled away the stone and sat upon it. The guards shook for fear of him and became like dead men (Matthew 28:4). Later, the guards reported back to the chief priests and told them what had happened. The chief priests paid off the soldiers to spread a lie that

Jesus' followers had stolen the body while they were asleep (Matthew 28:11-15).

Is it possible the disciples stole the body? Again, the evidence says no! The group of Roman guards was highly trained. They were cold-blooded killers and probably from the same group that crucified Jesus. They thought nothing of gambling for His clothes as He hung dying. The idea that a group of fishermen overpowered such guards is ridiculous. The Romans were professionals armed to the hilt. Also, there is no way they would have fallen asleep. The Roman army had eighteen offenses punishable by death. Two were for sleeping on watch or leaving a night watch. The guards would have been beating each other over the head to stay awake if they thought they might fall asleep!

6. The Seal on the Grave (Matthew 27:65,66)

The sixth reason the resurrection is true involves the "seal" placed on Christ's tomb. The seal was made by means of a cord or rope passing across the mouth of the tomb and fastened at either end with sealing clay. The seal represented the power of Rome. To break the Roman seal meant crucifixion upside down. The certainty of this punishment would put fear in the heart of anyone who thought about stealing the body. It is unthinkable that the disciples who fled and denied knowing Jesus for fear of a beating would tamper with a sealed grave and try to overpower the armed guard on penalty of death!

7. The Stone (Matthew 27:59,60, Mark 15:46).

The seventh reason the resurrection is true deals with the stone that was rolled in front of the entrance to the tomb. The purpose of the stone was to protect the dead body from man and beast. The wealthier the deceased, the bigger the stone. Because Jesus' tomb belonged to a rich man, Joseph of Arimathea, the stone was undoubtedly large. Scripture clearly indicates this, based on the account of the three women who came early on Sunday morning to anoint Jesus' body. They were concerned about who would move the stone (Mark 16:1-3). The stone was evidently too big for the three of them to manage by themselves.

Often, when a stone was placed in front of a tomb, it was rolled into place by pushing it down a groove using a lever and fulcrum. The groove normally went downhill. Placing the stone in front of a tomb entrance was relatively easy. Removing it proved nearly impossible. The stone would have to be rolled uphill. Some scholars estimate that the stone in front of Jesus' tomb may have weighed more than a ton.

Even if all the guards did fall asleep (which is highly unlikely), the disciples could never have moved such a large stone without waking them up. This is another reason why the disciples could not have stolen the body. The stone was removed for our benefit, not Christ's. It was removed by the angel so we could see in, not so Jesus could get out!

8. The Testimony of an Angel (Matthew 28:1-7)

On Sunday, the first day of the week, Mary Magdalene and the other Mary went to look at the grave. When they arrived, they saw the stone had been rolled away. An angel met them and said,

Do not be afraid; for I know that you are looking for Jesus who has been crucified. He is not here, for He has risen, just as He said. Come, see the place where He was lying. Go quickly and tell His disciples that He has risen from the dead; and behold, He is going ahead of you into Galilee, there you will see Him; behold, I have told you. Angels from God don't lie. Jesus had risen from the dead.

9. The Empty Tomb and Grave Clothes (John 20:3-8)

One theory that attempts to disprove the resurrection says the officials moved the body for safekeeping. If this was the case, all the officials needed to do was to parade Christ's dead body through the streets when word reached them that people thought He had risen from the dead. This would have quickly quelled any notion of a resurrection. They could not display the body because they didn't have it. The fact that the authorities tried to fabricate a story about the disciples stealing the body is an admission that the tomb stood empty.

Not only was the grave empty but the grave clothes lay empty. John 20:4-7 indicates they were like a cocoon. The only logical explanation is that Christ passed through them as He rose. The empty grave clothes show the supernatural nature of the resurrection.

10. Christ's Appearances (John 20:19-29, Acts 1:1-4)

Other powerful evidences for the resurrection are Jesus' many appearances after He rose from the dead. He appeared to individuals and crowds. On one such occasion, Thomas was absent. When the other disciples said they had seen Jesus, Thomas (doubting Thomas) refused to believe. Eight days later, Jesus appeared when Thomas was present and said to him,

Reach here with your finger, and see My hands; and reach here your hand and put it into My side; and do not be unbelieving, but believing. Thomas responded *My Lord and my God.*

Jesus appeared over a period of 40 days to numerous people. Some skeptics have tried to rationalize away these appearances as hallucinations, but this reasoning does not fit the evidence. Hallucinations tend to be personal. People in large groups don't have the same hallucination.

At one point, Jesus appeared to over 500 people. The disciples even saw Him ascend into heaven. Only an actual resurrection can adequately explain Jesus' many appearances.

11. The Changing of the Sabbath

The Jewish Sabbath was and still is totally sacred to the Jews. It is on Saturday. Jewish Christians changed their Sabbath to Sunday after Jesus rose from the dead. The only reason any of them would consider such a change would be if their leader, Jesus, actually rose on Sunday. That became the day to remember His miracle of conquering death.

12. Establishment of the Church

The twelfth reason why the resurrection is true involves the establishment of the Christian Church. After Christ rose, the church was established, and not even severe persecution could stop it. This speaks of an actual resurrection.

13. The Disciples' Changed Lives

The changed lives of the disciples offer perhaps the greatest evidence for the resurrection. The very men who ran away and denied Christ were now ready to die for Him. What caused such a drastic change? When they saw Him alive, they became convinced that He had conquered death. If He had conquered it, His promise of eternal life for all who trusted Him was also true. He was God.

People will die for what they believe to be true, even if it isn't. They will not, however, die for what they know is a lie. If the disciples had tried to fabricate the story of Jesus' resurrection, they would have stopped as soon as intense persecution began. Tradition tells us that all the disciples, except John, died martyrs' deaths. The only logical explanation for such change in the disciples' lives is an actual resurrection.

CONCLUDING REMARKS

The evidence strongly supports Jesus' resurrection as an historic fact. The evidence includes:

- Christ's own predictions
- History's testimony
- The fact that Jesus was dead
- The burial
- The guard
- The seal
- The stone
- The testimony of an angel
- The empty tomb and grave clothes
- Christ's appearances
- The changing of the Sabbath
- Establishment of the church
- The disciples' changed lives

Christ's resurrection was not a case where His heart stopped and started again after five minutes. He lay clinically dead for days.

The resurrection was a miracle and proof positive that He was and is part of the triune Godhead of Father, Son, and Holy Spirit.

In John 10:18, Jesus spoke about His life and said,

No one has taken it (My life) away from Me, but I lay it down on My own initiative. I have authority to lay it down, and I have authority to take it up again. This commandment I received from My Father.

When Jesus died on the cross, He did it of His own free will. He was not a helpless victim. No one took His life from Him; He gave it up willingly. Just as He laid it down, He took it up at the resurrection. Christ is risen, indeed!

DISCUSSION QUESTIONS

IS THE RESURRECTION TRUE?

1. Does any of the evidence for Jesus' resurrection seem especially strong to you? Explain.

2. Does any of the evidence for the resurrection of Jesus seem weak? Explain.

3. Why is the resurrection the crux of the Christian faith? What verse in the Bible makes this point clear?

4. What is the swoon theory? After going over the material in this lesson, would you agree or disagree with this theory?

5. In your own words, briefly explain each of the evidences for Jesus' resurrection found in this study.

- Christ's own predictions

- History's testimony

- The fact Jesus was dead

- The burial

- The guard

- The seal

- The stone

- The testimony of an angel

- The empty tomb and grave clothes

- Christ's appearances

- The changing of the Sabbath

- Establishment of the church

- The disciples' changed lives

6. What is your view of the resurrection, and how has this study affected it?

CHAPTER

FIVE

IF GOD EXISTS, WHY DO EVIL, SUFFERING, AND PAIN EXIST?

Murder, rape, starvation, and disease are just a few of the evils in the world today. People rightly ask, "If God exists, why would He allow these things? Doesn't He see what's going on? Isn't He strong enough to stop all the problems? Perhaps He's not loving and good after all..."

KEY PRELIMINARY QUESTIONS

1. Is God strong enough to stop evil?

One person put it this way, "For God to allow evil, suffering, and pain – either He must not be all-powerful, or He must not be all-good. Perhaps He wants to stop evil but can't. Or, perhaps, He's all-powerful but chooses not to stop it because He's not all-good. If He were all-good and all-powerful, surely He would put an end to the world's problems."

The inquiry regarding evil, suffering, and pain deserves a definitive response. The Bible teaches that God is all-powerful and all-good. Genesis 1:1 states that God created everything out of

104

nothing. To do so, He certainly is omnipotent (all-powerful). Regarding God's goodness, Psalm 100:5 states, *For the LORD is good; His lovingkindness is everlasting, and His faithfulness to all generations.* Based on this verse, God certainly is all-good.

Could it be that even though God is all-powerful and all-good, evil exists because God simply doesn't know what's going on? Psalm 139:1-4 dispels this argument,

O LORD, Thou hast searched me and known me. Thou dost know when I sit down and when I rise up; Thou dost understand my thought from afar. Thou dost scrutinize my path and my lying down, and art intimately acquainted with all my ways. Even before there is a word on my tongue, behold, O LORD, Thou dost know it all.

In these verses, David acknowledges that God knows everything. He knows our thoughts from afar. He knows what's on our minds before we open our mouths. He is in touch with everything that goes on in His creation. Matthew 10:29 states that not even a sparrow falls to the ground, apart from God knowing about it. The passage goes on to say God even knows the number of hairs on our heads. For some of us, it is getting easier for Him to count! Certainly, God knows everything, everywhere, all the time!

If God is all-powerful, all-loving, and all-knowing, why would He allow evil, suffering, and pain? To understand this fully, we must first understand the origin of evil.

2. Did God create evil?

Because the Bible teaches that God created all things, some people accuse God of creating evil. This notion runs contrary to the statements in Scripture that indicate everything God created is good (Genesis 1:4,10,12,18,21,25,31). Since God didn't create evil, where did it come from? Evil came when God's creatures, to whom He gave the ability to choose, chose not to follow or obey Him.

The dictionary defines evil as the opposite of good. Since God is the epitome of goodness, evil comes about when anyone goes against God's desires. For example, God's Word, the Bible, says people are not to murder each other. God places a high value on human life. When a person disobeys God's Word and murders someone, he has committed an evil act. Evil usually results in suffering and pain.

When God created angels in Heaven, He gave them the ability to choose. Satan, one of the most magnificent angels, desired to become like God and rebelled (Ezekiel 28:12-19). Satan's rebellion resulted in his expulsion from Heaven. He and other rebellious angels were cast down to the earth.

Satan's sin of arrogance is recorded in the five "I wills" of Isaiah 14:12-15.

> How you have fallen from heaven, O star of the morning, son of the dawn! You have been cut down to the earth... But you said in your heart, 'I will ascend to heaven; I will raise my throne above the stars of God, and I will sit on the mount of assembly in the recesses of the north. I will ascend above the heights of the clouds; I will make myself like the Most High.' Nevertheless, you will be thrust down to Sheol, to the recesses of the pit.

Satan is now completely evil – known by such titles as the Devil, Lucifer, Prince of the Power of the Air, Beelzebul, and Ruler of the Demons. The fallen angels, who were expelled from heaven with him, now serve as his demons. Together, they stir up spiritual trouble on the earth. Their activities go against God's will and are thus evil.

Some people ask, "Why doesn't God forgive the angels and welcome them back?" Scripture doesn't say. Perhaps it is because God is holy and just and can't have sin around Him. Perhaps it's because the angels were in His presence when they rebelled, giving them no excuse for their actions.

Others ask, "If Satan and his cohorts did such an evil thing, why didn't God destroy them immediately? Why did He cast them down to the earth and give them the opportunity to influence humans? Again, the Bible does not tell us. Perhaps God wanted to demonstrate, in the end, that goodness wins out over evil.

Regarding evil, it is important to understand a time is coming when God will destroy it. Satan and his demons will eventually be cast into the Lake of Fire (Hell) and remain there forever (Matthew 25:41, Revelation 20:10). Revelation 21:4 describes what it will be like when God ushers in the New Heaven and the New Earth, *And He will wipe away every tear from their eyes; and there will no longer be any death; there will no longer be any mourning, or crying, or pain; the first things have passed away.*

In our world where evil, suffering, and pain are rampant, many people long for the time when God makes everything right. Why doesn't God usher in the end right now? We don't know. We do know His timing is perfect. The restoration may happen in our lifetime, or it may be in a future generation – but it is coming. This is one of the great hopes of all who trust God.

3. What about evil and humans?

When God created humans, He gave them the ability to choose, just as He did the angels. For Adam and Eve, the choice came when God said, *From any tree of the garden you may eat freely; but from the tree of the knowledge of good and evil you shall not eat, for in the day that you eat from it you will surely die.* (Genesis 2:16,17)

After Satan tempted them, Adam and Eve disobeyed God and ate the forbidden fruit. This resulted in their expulsion from the Garden of Eden and their own spiritual death. Although God did not kill them physically, they died spiritually, and their physical aging clocks started ticking. Adam and Eve's years on earth were now numbered. At the same time, God promised that one day He would send a Savior through the seed of the woman to crush the power of Satan and set things right (Genesis 3:15). This was the first prophecy concerning the coming Messiah, Jesus.

Did God create evil? No! Instead, He created choice. When God created angels and humans, He gave them the ability to make moral choices. When some of the angels and Adam and Eve made the wrong choices, evil was born bringing with it suffering and pain. Since the fall, the world has never been the same.

4. Why did God create choice?

God could have made angels and humans like robots to do right all the time. He didn't because He wanted them to have a personal relationship with Him. In other words, God wanted them to worship and serve Him just because they wanted to, not because they were programmed to. Without choice, no meaningful relationship could exist.

Consider marriage as a way to understand the importance of choice in relationships. Choice serves as one of the most powerful ingredients in a husband-wife relationship; each spouse chooses to love the other. No thinking husband would want a robot for a wife (at least not for long), nor would a wife want a robot for a husband. The fact a man chooses his wife above all other women makes her feel special, and vice versa. It gives the relationship meaning and purpose. But choice also carries the greatest danger; one spouse can stop loving the other, have an affair, or file for divorce. The benefits of a loving relationship, however, far outweigh the risks. So it is with God and people. He gives people a choice. They can follow Him or go their own willful way. Some people will follow, and some will not. Those who follow receive His blessing. Those who disobey suffer the negative consequences of their own choices.

When people choose to rebel against God, they, not God, bear the full responsibility for their actions. Unfortunately, people's choices often affect others. When a man chooses to drink and drive, he may accidentally kill someone in the process. When a wife chooses to commit adultery, she may emotionally scar her children. When a businessman chooses to be dishonest in order to make more money, he may find it backfires and destroys his company, leaving many innocent employees out of work.

Certainly, God could step in and stop the ripple effect of evil. Undoubtedly, there are times He does. But He often allows people's choices to play themselves out, hoping the outcome will wake people up, causing them to turn to Him.

Regarding God's divine protection, I remember the time as a young boy when my friend and I were at the dairy farm his father managed. We were playing in a barn under construction. As we explored the unfinished facility, we decided to hide some tools (a wrench, pliers, and screwdriver) in a small opening in the wall. Not realizing the opening was an uncovered electrical outlet with live wires, we dropped the tools in the hole and went out to ride our bikes. When we returned, my friend reached into the opening, felt a weird sensation, and was unable to get the tools. I told him I could get the tools. When I reached in, I felt the same sensation. We decided to leave the tools there and tell his dad.

Looking back on the incident, both of us should have died. Some might say our rubber boots saved us. More likely, it was God's hand of mercy.

Although many folks die in tragedies every day, there are

countless others who are spared because of God's intervention. The September 11, 2001, tragedy at the World Trade Center is one example. The evil of a few affected the lives of many. Although thousands died, many others were spared. Undoubtedly, God was at work for good, even amidst man's evil. Why did some die while others were spared? No one knows for sure. The answer will likely remain a mystery this side of Heaven.

In summary, evil is a result of choice. Wrong choices often bring pain and suffering, not only to those who do evil but to those around it. One day, God will eliminate evil and the resulting pain and suffering. In the meantime, we must remember that we live in a fallen world.

With these preliminary thoughts, let's now look at several reasons why there is "suffering and pain" in the world. We'll even see how God sometimes uses these for good.

REASONS WHY THERE IS "PAIN AND SUFFERING"

1. The natural world has been affected by sin

Adam's sin affected all people; it affected the entire created world. Romans 8:19-23 explains:

> *For the anxious longing of the creation waits eagerly for the revealing of the sons of God. For the creation was subjected to futility, not of its own will, but because of Him who subjected it, in hope that the creation itself also will be set free from its slavery to corruption into the freedom of the glory of the children of God. For we know that the whole creation groans and suffers the pains of childbirth together until now.*

At first reading this passage may sound a bit obscure, but it refers to the fact that sin not only affected humans, it affected all creation. Part of the curse when Adam sinned fell upon the earth. Genesis 3:17-18 states, *Then to Adam He [God] said, "Because you have listened to the voice of your wife, and have eaten from the tree about which I commanded you, saying, 'You shall not eat from it;' Cursed is the ground because of you; In toil you shall eat of it all the days of your life. Both thorns and thistles it shall grow for you..."*

Ever since the creation was cursed, the physical world has groaned for its Redeemer. Some of the natural phenomena (earthquakes, tidal waves, etc.) in the world are part of that groaning. Like a ship creaking in a violent sea, like a house straining in a powerful storm, like a mother groaning in childbirth, so the creation creaks, strains, and groans, awaiting God's salvation and the ushering in of a New Heaven and Earth. Some of this groaning takes the form of natural disasters. It is true that hurricanes, tornadoes, earthquakes, tidal waves, volcanoes, and other disasters, as well as cancer and other diseases, can be explained scientifically. But when God ushers in the New Heavens and Earth free from sin, these things will vanish. They are here because we live in a fallen world.

Another effect of the fall is the aging process. People grow old, body functions fail, and parts wear out. It is fairly easy to tell the approximate ages of people. Those in their teens look different than those in their thirties. Middle-aged folks look different than those who are sixty and older. Wrinkles and gray hair tell the story. Why do old people die? Sometimes, their bodies simply wear out! It will happen to each of us if we live long enough. But thanks be to God who promises to give Christians new bodies that will never wear out (1 Corinthians 15:50-57).

In a sin-affected world where God's perfect creation is tarnished, suffering and pain happen. Some people may object and say, "Why doesn't God do something about it?" He has! He sent Christ to die for our sins so that we can be forgiven if we place our trust in Him. In addition, He will take us to be with Him for eternity after we die. In the meantime, we all must suffer under the curse of sin brought on by our ancestors. But rest assured, God will have the last word!

2. Physical laws have been violated

A second reason why there is "pain and suffering" is because people violate God's physical laws. Just as God established spiritual laws to govern the spiritual realm, so He established physical laws to govern the physical world. One such law deals with time and space. In brief, "Two things cannot occupy the same space at the same time."

I will never forget, as a child in elementary school running back from the playground to my classroom. I was looking back over my shoulder, yelling something to a friend, when a sudden thud sent me reeling. I had run right into a pole that supported the overhang outside the building. My head and the pole could not occupy the same space at the same time. The pole won! This incident did not cause too much pain and suffering, but when the same principle is applied to automobiles and pedestrians, snow skiers and trees, or the ground and airplanes, it quickly becomes a tragedy of immense proportions.

Other laws, such as gravity and centrifugal force, make it necessary to avoid jumping from high places or driving too fast around corners.

Think for a minute about the San Francisco earthquake and the collapse of part of the Nimitz Freeway. The builders of the freeway knew about the potential forces inherent in a major earthquake and chose (perhaps for financial reasons) not to build their structure to withstand such forces. Their choice led to disaster. Sadly, many things are built on the low bid. Galatians 6:7 reads, *Do not be deceived, God is not mocked; for whatever a man sows, this he will also reap.*

As humans, God has given us incredible intellects that are constantly unlocking more knowledge about His creation. When new discoveries are made, human applications must be in harmony with God's physical laws. If we build taller buildings, faster planes, or more sophisticated equipment, they must not violate known principles. To do so is to invite disaster. God is not likely to change His laws just because people decide to violate them. That would go against His holy and righteous character. The result of disobedience, whether intentional or unintentional, is often tragic. We reap what we sow.

3. People choosing to sin

Undoubtedly, sin brings tragedy, not only original sin, but the sinful choices people make every day. When people knowingly choose to violate God's standards, pain and suffering often follow.

When I was serving as an Air Force chaplain, a man came for counseling and told me he had killed his wife. I asked him to explain what he meant, and he told me he had not actually killed her, but she was probably as good as dead. He had been stationed at a remote site away from his family and was only able to visit them once every several months. While at the remote location, he got emotionally and physically involved with another woman. When he went home on vacation, he slept with his wife as if nothing was wrong. When he returned to duty, the woman with whom he was having an affair informed him that she had just tested positive for HIV. It was likely he also would test positive and had passed it on to his wife. Through tears, he asked me what to do. Should he tell his wife or wait to see if she contracted AIDS?

All through the Bible, there are accounts of sin bringing negative consequences. In Acts 5, Ananias and Sapphira sinned when they lied to the Holy Spirit. As a warning to the early church, God struck them dead. Does God always make examples of people when they sin? No. If He did, none of us would be alive. But rest assured, sin often leads to pain and suffering. James 4:1-11 makes this point clear; *What is the source of quarrels and conflicts among you? Is not the source your pleasures that wage war in your members? You lust and do not have; so you commit murder. And you are envious and cannot obtain; you fight and quarrel.* Lust can lead to murder. Envy can lead to fights.

As mentioned earlier, sin often affects more than the one who commits the sin. The so-called "innocent bystander" is usually impacted, too. Think of the story of Jonah in the Old Testament. When Jonah ran from God, he boarded a ship heading in the opposite direction from where God wanted him to go. Subsequently, God caused a violent storm, resulting in Jonah's expulsion from the ship and his subsequent ride inside the stomach of a great fish. The people on the ship had not caused God's wrath, but they endured considerable hardship because of Jonah's sinful choices. Their cargo was jettisoned and lost in an attempt to save the ship. Indeed, Jonah's sin touched everyone around him.

Just as God causes the rain to fall on the righteous and unrighteous, so the results of sin have an extraordinary ripple effect. In a world torn apart by sin – people kill each other, nations go to war, people get raped, and drunks have car wrecks. To say this is true is not pessimistic; it is harsh reality.

It is also important to understand there actually are no "innocent bystanders." All of us are sinners and deserve God's judgment. We should not be asking, "Why are there so many tragedies in the world?" But, instead, "Why are there so few per capita when people willfully and constantly sin against the One who gave them the precious gift of life?"

Regarding God's gracious protection, the Bible teaches that Christians have guardian angels (Psalm 34:7, Matthew 18:10, Hebrews 1:14). If the truth were known, those who genuinely love God, and even those who do not love God, have been saved from disaster on many occasions.

Another bit of great news is, even if God chooses not to protect believers from physical harm, their home in Heaven is secure!

4. The direct intervention of Satan

Another reason why there is suffering and pain in the world has to do with the direct intervention of Satan. Just as God wants to build lives, Satan wants to destroy them. The Bible contains the story of Job. He was God's faithful servant. Satan came to God and said, in essence, the only reason Job served God was because Job had so much material wealth. Satan was sure if Job's wealth was removed, Job would turn away from God (Job 1:6-11).

God allowed Satan to test Job. As a result, Job went through horrendous difficulties: his flocks were destroyed, his family killed, and his personal health ruined. Although in the end, God restored everything (and then some) to Job, Satan did try to destroy Job.

Perhaps some of the tough times you have experienced were because Satan or his demons were trying to drag you down. If so, don't give in! Have the same attitude as Job, who said, *Though He (God) slay me, I will hope in Him.* (Job 13:15).

HOW CAN GOD USE PAIN AND SUFFERING FOR GOOD?

Not only is there pain and suffering in the world, the good news is God can use it for good. Romans 8:28 states, *And we know that God causes all things to work together for good to those who love God, to those who are called according to His purpose.*

Sometimes, God uses pain and suffering in one of the following ways.

1. As a test

James 1:2-5 says, *Consider it all joy, my brethren, when you encounter various trials, knowing that the testing of your faith produces endurance. And let endurance have its perfect result, that you may be perfect and complete, lacking in nothing.*

There are times when God will take us through a trial or period of suffering to strengthen us. There is a misconception in some Christian circles that believers are never supposed to suffer. In Philippians 1:29, Paul states otherwise; *For to you it has been granted for Christ's sake not only to believe in Him, but also to suffer for His sake...* Suffering is part of God's will for the Christian. Because we are sinners, suffering helps us remember that this world is not our home, and we need to trust God. It also helps us identify with Christ's sufferings.

In 1 Peter 4:12-14 the apostle Peter said,

Beloved, do not be surprised at the fiery ordeal among you, which comes upon you for your testing, as though some strange thing were happening to you; but to the degree that you share the sufferings of Christ, keep on rejoicing; so that also at the revelation of His glory, you may rejoice with exultation. If you are reviled for the name of Christ, you are blessed, because the Spirit of glory and of God rests upon you.

The recipients of Peter's letter were experiencing great suffering. If a person reads all of 1 Peter, the whole book is about suffering and Peter's encouragement to people to hang tough. Although some of the recipients of this letter obviously looked upon their suffering as tragic, Peter informed them it was only a test. God was using it for their good.

Just as a track coach strengthens his runners through the pain of intensive weight workouts and grueling runs, so God sometimes allows us to suffer in order to strengthen our faith. Remember, His intentions are good. Make up your mind to pass the test!

2. To keep a person from exalting himself

Scripture indicates God will allow us to suffer to save us from our own selfishness and pride. Such was the case with Paul. In 2 Corinthians 12:7-10 Paul said,

And because of the surpassing greatness of the revelations, for this reason, to keep me from exalting myself, there was given me a thorn in the flesh, a messenger of Satan to buffet me – to keep me from exalting myself! Concerning this I entreated the Lord three times that it might depart from me. And He has said to me, "My grace is sufficient for you, for power is perfected in weakness." Most gladly, therefore, I will rather boast about my weaknesses, that the power of Christ may dwell in me.

God knows if we have a tendency toward pride. He wants us to be strong in Him, not in ourselves. For this reason, He may allow suffering or pain to touch our lives.

3. To further the Gospel

When people wind up in prison for no good reason, it seems tragic. Such was the case with the apostle Paul. He was placed in jail for sharing God's plan of salvation. But God had a purpose in Paul's imprisonment: to further the Gospel and to strengthen

Paul's fellow believers. Listen to Paul's words in Philippians 1:12-14,

> *Now I want you to know, brethren, that my circumstances have turned out for the greater progress of the gospel, so that my imprisonment in the cause of Christ has become well known throughout the whole praetorian guard and to everyone else, and that most of the brethren, trusting in the Lord because of my imprisonment have far more courage to speak the Word of God without fear.*

The question becomes, "Are we ready and willing to suffer for the sake of the Gospel?"

Paul had a great ministry of church planting, but God had bigger plans. He wanted Paul to start a prison ministry. When God allowed Paul to go to prison, He knew many people would come to Christ through Paul's witness. Paul was happy to be part of spreading the Gospel even further.

How would you feel if you were imprisoned for your faith? It happens all the time in different parts of the world. Would you complain and turn away from God, or would you praise Him and use your imprisonment as an opportunity to spread His Word?

What about illness? Would you still trust God if He allowed you to get a disease if that's what it took to jar your relatives or friends out of their spiritual apathy? It is correctly said, "Man's calamity is God's opportunity." Not only do many people come to Christ through their own crises but also through the crises of loved ones or friends.

I have wrestled with the concept of death for a long time. I know I will die – we all will. But I have asked myself if I am willing to go through suffering and pain in my own life to bring some of my unsaved family to Christ. I don't cherish the thought, but I am willing if that's what it takes. After all, if Christians die, they go to heaven. If non-Christians die, they go to hell. There is no amount of suffering in this life that a Christian can go through that compares to the suffering in the next life that those who die without Christ will experience. In like manner, there is no amount of suffering in this life that Christians can go through that compares with the glories they will receive in heaven. That's why Romans 8:18 states, *For I consider that the sufferings of this present time are not worthy to be compared with the glory that is to be revealed to us.* Christians should, therefore, be willing to suffer hardship for the sake of the gospel.

4. For God's greater glory

Another reason why God may allow pain and suffering to touch our lives is for His greater glory. This is very closely linked to the preceding category. A good example is found in John chapter nine, which records the story of a man born blind.

Jesus' disciples were concerned why the man had been born blind. Was it because of his sin or his parents' sin? Jesus answered in verse three, *It was neither that this man sinned, nor his parents; but it was in order that the works of God might be displayed in him.* In other words, God allowed this man to suffer so God's power could be displayed in a special way at the proper time.

You may ask, "Does God allow people to go through pain and suffering if it will bring greater good? Yes. God is the potter; we are the clay (Romans 9:14-21). His thoughts and ways are higher than ours (Isaiah 55:8,9). We can know, even if tragedy strikes, God can work it to His glory and touch lives for His kingdom.

What was the result of the man being healed of blindness? He eventually came to Christ and was a witness to others. Even though the Pharisees rejected the man's witness, many people recognized the miracle and glorified God.

One of the best modern-day examples of "God's greater glory" is what happened to Joni Erickson Tada. As a teenager, she dove into a lake, broke her neck, and became quadriplegic. Many people look at this as a great tragedy, but through Joni, God has touched many people who probably never would have been reached if this event had not happened. Joni writes books, paints by holding a paintbrush with her teeth, hosts a daily nationwide radio program, and is an unbelievable example of courage. Not only have many people come to Christ through Joni's tragedy, but many Christians have been encouraged to press on amidst their own suffering. And through it all, God has been glorified.

5. To teach us something

The Bible records the story of Lazarus, one of Jesus' good friends. John chapter 11 says Lazarus was sick, and his sisters sent a message to Jesus to come quickly, hoping He would heal their brother. Jesus delayed two extra days, and Lazarus died. When Jesus approached Lazarus' hometown, He was met by Martha, Lazarus' sister. Martha was distraught and shared with Jesus that her brother would not have died if Jesus had come sooner. Jesus subsequently raised Lazarus from the dead and used the sequence of events to teach Lazarus' sisters and the disciples an important lesson, "Jesus had the power to raise the dead and was and is the resurrection and the life."

God may allow tragedy to touch our lives in order to teach us something.

6. For the good of others

The story of Joseph in the Old Testament is a classic example of God using tragedy for the good of others. The account is found in

Genesis 37-50. Joseph had a coat of many colors his father had given to him. Joseph loved the Lord but had several jealous brothers who hated him and sold him into slavery. He was subsequently falsely accused of rape and wrongfully thrown into prison. A person who promised to get him out of prison forgot about him. Joseph's life was one undeserved tragedy after another. The unusual thing about Joseph was he never turned from God but kept trusting. To make a long story short, God used Joseph, a Jew, to interpret the dream of the Egyptian Pharaoh. Joseph was subsequently released from prison and quickly promoted to second in command of all Egypt. In this position, God used him to store grain during plentiful years and then meet the food needs of the nation of Israel during famine years. Joseph was allowed to go through years of suffering so Israel might be preserved. Strangely enough, Joseph helped the same brothers who sold him into slavery.

God may take us through times of pain and suffering for the good of others and possibly even for the good of those responsible for our suffering.

7. To save someone from greater judgment

The account of Sodom and Gomorrah is another example of God working to bring good out of evil.

There are so many things to learn from the account of Sodom and Gomorrah found in Genesis 19. Here is a quick summary of the story: Two angels were sent to Sodom and Gomorrah to rescue Lot and his family before the cities were destroyed. When the angels arrived in Sodom, the perverted townspeople demanded that Lot send out the angelic visitors to have sexual relations with them. When Lot refused, the people of Sodom tried to break down Lot's door. God then struck the people with blindness. Even so, Genesis 19:11 states, *They wearied themselves trying to find the doorway.*

Can you imagine how perverted these townspeople were? Even when struck with blindness, they still wanted to carry out their evil, lustful desires.

When tragedy strikes, people sometimes review their lives to determine if their suffering is a result of sin. If sin is present, the people often repent. The people in Sodom and Gomorrah refused to repent. Instead, even in blindness, they pressed on with their evil intentions no matter how hard God tried to dissuade them.

What did the people of these two corrupt cities deserve? Death! Why did God simply blind them instead of destroying them on the spot? He did it to demonstrate His love and patience and to give the people one more chance to repent. 2 Peter 3:9 states, *The Lord is not slow about His promises, as some count slowness, but is patient toward you, not wishing for any to perish but for all to come to repentance.*

Because the people of Sodom and Gomorrah refused to repent, judgment fell, and their cities and all the inhabitants were destroyed.

There are times when God may allow hardship to touch our lives in small measure, hoping we will repent so He doesn't have to lower the boom. In such instances, the "pain and suffering" is a true act of God's love.

God is not responsible for evil in the world. Evil is the result of sinful choices. Unfortunately, wrong choices often lead to pain and/or suffering, which may have a ripple effect on the lives of others. The good news is, God can bring good out of pain and suffering, and one day, will eliminate them completely.

DISCUSSION QUESTIONS

IF GOD EXISTS, WHY DO "EVIL, SUFFERING, AND PAIN EXIST?"

1. In the past, what has been your view on the existence of evil, suffering and pain in the world?

2. According to this study, did God create evil? Explain.

3. Why is choice an important part of relationships? Why did God create angels and humans with the ability to choose?

4. What are some of the reasons, according to the Bible, why suffering and pain exist in the world?

5. How does God use pain and suffering for good? Give examples.

6. How has the information in this booklet affected your view of evil, suffering, and pain?

CHAPTER

SIX

HAS SCIENCE DISPROVED THE BIBLE? IS EVOLUTION TRUE?

S ome people think science has long since disproved the Bible. With the advent of evolution, they feel those who believe the Bible must commit intellectual suicide and turn their backs on scientific facts. But is this true? Must a person stick his head in the sands of ignorance in order to embrace the teachings of Scripture? Check the evidence and decide for yourself.

The purpose of this study is to shed light on the subject of science and the Bible and to take a close look at the evolution-creation debate. Once a person looks honestly at the evidence, he can make informed decisions about what to believe.

SCIENCE AND THE BIBLE

Although the Bible is not primarily a science book, when it speaks about scientific things, it does so with amazing accuracy.

Throughout history, the scientific world has pointed an accusing finger at the Bible, saying it contains scientific errors. Time has shown science to be wrong, and the Bible to be correct.

One example is the number of stars. Before the telescope was invented in the 17th century, astronomers believed there were approximately 1000 stars. Ptolemy put the number at 1,056. Tycho Brahe catalogued 777 stars. Kepler believed there were 1,005.[1]

With the invention of the telescope, we now know there are more than 100 billion stars in our own galaxy and billions of galaxies besides our own. Jeremiah 33:22 states, *the host of heaven cannot be counted...* This statement refers to the number of stars in the heavens. The Bible says the number is beyond our ability to count. This is totally accurate since many of the other galaxies are so far away that the stars in them cannot be individually distinguished even with the best telescopes. The galaxies simply look like a cloud of light. Indeed the farther we look into space, the more galaxies we discover. It is interesting how long it took science to catch up with the Bible.

Another example of the scientific accuracy of the Bible comes from Job 26:7 which states *He (God) hangs the earth on nothing.* The idea the earth hangs in space by itself sounds like scientific talk from the 21st century. Although scientists did not believe this until more recent times, the Bible has taught it for thousands of years.

A third example of the Bible's scientific accuracy is found in Isaiah 40:22. It reads, *It is He who sits above the circle of the earth...* The Hebrew word for circle is 'chuwg' which can be translated sphericity or roundness. Until modern times, people believed the world was flat. The Bible has always taught it is round. Again, it took time for science to catch up. [2]

A fourth example is found in Job 36:27,28 and Ecclesiastes 1:6-7. These passages explain the winds and the hydrologic processes of evaporation, condensation, and precipitation. This explanation is

---

1. Henry M. Morris, *The Bible and Modern Science*, (Moody Press, 1967), 5.
2. 2 Ibid., p. 6.

miraculous considering these facts were not clearly understood until more recent times. [3]

The sanitation and dietary laws of Moses recorded in Leviticus also show the scientific accuracy of the Bible. Certain foods were considered unclean, and the Jews were forbidden to eat them. Other foods were considered clean and fit for human consumption. We now know there were good reasons for obeying these laws.

Also, God commanded the Jews to follow a certain procedure for disposing of human excrement (Deuteronomy 23:12-14). They were to take it outside the camp and bury it. This procedure saved the Jews from many diseases that plagued other cultures. If people in Europe during the Middle Ages had obeyed this one sanitation law, and not dumped human excrement out their windows into the street, they might have saved themselves from various plagues that were undoubtedly fueled by the presence of raw human feces. [4]

In addition, Genesis 17:12 states, *And every male among you who is eight days old shall be circumcised throughout your generations.* In the last century, science has discovered that circumcision is a valuable health practice. The Bible has encouraged the circumcision of male children for thousands of years. In addition, the Bible said males were to be circumcised on the eighth day. It is now known that two important clotting elements, vitamin K and prothrombin, are at their peak on day eight, thus helping to prevent hemorrhaging and subsequent infection. How did the ancient Jews know to circumcise their male children at just the right time? God told them! [5]

It is important to realize that science and the Bible are not incompatible. In fact, there are many scientists today who believe in God and see no contradiction between science and Scripture. They

---

3. Ibid., p. 7-8.
4. Ibid., p.9.
5. S.I. McMillen and David E. Stern, *None of These Diseases,* (Fleming and Revell Company, 1984), 87-96

have followed in the footsteps of countless others, including Albert Einstein.

KEY PRELIMINARY QUESTIONS

1. Is evolution a proven scientific fact?

With the widespread belief in evolution, many people think they must believe it or be labeled ignorant. They are under the impression that evolution is a scientific fact. The truth is, the jury is still out. It is thus the purpose of this chapter to ask and answer many of the questions surrounding the evolution-creation debate, so that people can make informed decisions regarding which theory they should believe. Today, the theory of evolution is under fire not only by creation scientists but also by some of its own advocates. After over a century and countless dollars spent trying to prove the theory, evolutionists are still at a loss to present any compelling evidence regarding its validity.

Not only are there many scientists who do not believe in evolution, many of them have devoted their lives to showing its fallacies. Some of these scientists are associated with organizations like The Institute For Creation Research in Texas, or Answers In Genesis in Kentucky.

Physicist Dr. Robert Millikan, a Nobel Prize winner said, "To me it is unthinkable that a real atheist could be a scientist."[6] Why? Because the whole universe is bulging with evidence that someone with great intelligence designed it. Many scientists believe that someone is God.

There are even scientists who have been long-time advocates of

---

6. Edward F. Blick, *Correlation of the Bible and Science* (Southwest Radio Church, 1988), 3.

evolution who now say the theory is bankrupt. Rather than further research confirming the theory, it is undermining it.

Three of the best books written in recent years showing the lack of evidence for evolution are "Darwin's Black Box" by Michael Behe, "Evolution a Theory in Crisis" by Michael Denton, and "Darwin on Trial" by Phillip Johnson. If a person wants to see even more information, books, and videos on the subject, he should go to:

www.icr.org (icr = The Institute for Creation Research),

www.explorationfilms.com,

www.AnswersInGenesis.org on the internet.

2. Is evolution true science, and creation just religion?

Neither evolution nor creation can be proven scientifically. Why? Because neither can be subjected to the scientific method of direct observation and analysis. True science involves things that are observable, measurable and repeatable for verification. Neither evolution nor creation fit into this category. No human was there to observe how the universe or life began. For that matter, no one in the past or present has ever seen macroevolution take place (macro and micro-evolution will be defined later). Advocates of evolution or creation believe their theories based on the available circumstantial evidence or their own personal faith. That is why many people say evolution and creation border on religion. Creationists put their faith in God. Evolutionists put their faith in chance. Both creationists and evolutionists have the same evidence. They simply interpret it differently.

Christians, however, do claim to have one overwhelming line of evidence, but this, too, requires faith. They believe God was there at the beginning of time and shares in His Word, the Bible, how the universe and the earth began.

It must be said that a person's belief in evolution or creation is often closely linked with his preconceived biases. In other words, if a person does not believe in God, he has great difficulty believing the creation theory, no matter how strong the evidence. On the flip side, people who believe in God have no difficulty believing the creation theory, even if it cannot be proven scientifically. A person's bias, either for or against God, makes a huge difference in the conclusions he draws.

Whether or not you believe in God, you are encouraged to look at the following evidence with an open mind. If you are currently an evolutionist, you may come away with a whole new appreciation for the theory of creation. Before looking at the evidence, let's first answer a few more important questions.

3. If evolution is not a fact, why do so many people believe it?

Many people believe evolution because they were taught it in school, heard it in the media (television, radio, or movies), read it in a book or magazine, or saw it depicted at a museum. When asked to give reasons why they believe, most people are at a loss other than to say, "Evolution must be true because that is what the majority of people believe. If evolution wasn't true, wouldn't someone tell us?" The following material will hopefully shed some light on this question. People need to remember: the majority is not always right. For centuries the majority of people believed the world was flat.

4. Are evolution or creation the only possibilities for origins?

Evolution and creation are the only two possibilities for origins. Either a supernatural power created everything, or it all evolved by random chance. There are no other viable options. Some people believe in theistic evolution (a combination of the two), but it will be shown that the Bible does not leave room for this option.

Some scientists speculate that life came to earth via cosmic dust or aliens, but this raises another question, "Where did these life forms originate? Were they created or did they evolve?"

Since both evolution and creation are theories. The question becomes, "Which theory is best supported by the evidence?" Although evolutionists say their theory carries the most weight, many excellent scientists disagree. And the number of scientists who reject evolution is growing.

5. Is the evolution-creation debate really that important?

The evolution-creation debate is vitally important! Many people have turned away or stayed away from believing in God because they think evolution has made the whole concept of God obsolete. After all, if evolution is true, God did not create the universe as the Bible claims. If this biblical claim is false, then the Bible cannot be trusted and must be discarded as irrelevant.

If, on the other hand, creation is true, the Bible's claim that God created everything is also true. If this claim is true, then it is likely the rest of the Bible is true. If the whole Bible is true, then it needs to be embraced as the handbook for life and salvation.

With these thoughts in mind, let's now define the various areas of evolution and examine the evidence. When looked at with a discerning mind it is clear that the evidence supports the theory of creation as well as, if not better than, the theory of evolution.

WHAT ARE THE VARIOUS AREAS OF EVOLUTION?

There are three basic areas of evolution. The first is *cosmic evolution* which addresses the origin of the universe. Those who believe in cosmic evolution believe the universe came into being by natural means. The second area is chemical evolution. It addresses the origin of the first forms of life. Those who believe in chemical evolution believe first-life on earth came into being by natural means. The third area is biological evolution. This theory addresses the origin of new life forms from existing ones. Those who believe in biological evolution believe that all currently existing species of plants and animals have developed from previously existing species through a gradual process known as natural selection.[7]

Although each area will be addressed in this study, the greatest emphasis will be given to biological evolution because it is the one area most people think of when the subject of evolution is mentioned. Let's begin with cosmic evolution.

IS COSMIC EVOLUTION TRUE?

Again, cosmic evolution is the belief that the universe originated through natural means. Does the evidence support this notion? Decide for yourself.

1. The First Law of Thermodynamics and the Principle of Causality

Most scientists who believe in cosmic evolution believe matter is eternal and the universe has always existed. They base their belief on the First Law of Thermodynamics known as the law of energy conservation. This law states, "Energy can neither be created nor destroyed." In other words the total amount of actual energy in the universe remains constant. Energy can drift from one object to

---

7. Norman L. Geisler, *Baker Encyclopedia of Christian Apologetics*, (Baker Books, 1999), 224.

another – like when hot coffee warms up a cold mug. Energy can be converted into mechanical work – like when gasoline in a car engine is burned and converted into power to drive the pistons. Energy can also be stored – like in a piece of firewood. That energy is released when the wood is set on fire. But, the energy cannot be destroyed. It simply changes form.

Although the First Law of Thermodynamics applies perfectly to the physical universe, it does not address the ultimate question of energy's origin. Because the First Law of Thermodynamics fails to answer the question of origins, it violates an equally valid physical law, the Principle of Causality.

The Principle of Causality states that every effect has a cause. In other words, for energy to exist, it had to come from somewhere. It could not have simply shown up.

Since both the First Law of Thermodynamics and the Principle of Causality are equally true in the physical world, and yet the Principle of Causality contradicts the notion of an eternal universe, which principle is actually true? They both are! In order to reconcile both, a person is forced to the logical conclusion that both came into existence after a power outside the universe created the universe. Christians call that power, God.

Another way to explain Causality (cause and effect) and how it connects to the supernatural realm is as follows. We live in a time-space-matter continuum. In order for each of these to exist in the present (the effect), they had to have a beginning (a cause). For example, if matter did not have a beginning, then a person would go back forever trying to find its origin. If he went back forever, there would be no starting point from which to come forward to the present. This would mean that matter could not exist in the present. But matter does exist in the present, thus making it impossible for matter, as we know it, to be eternal. Matter, then, had to have a beginning. The same is true for time and space. Both must have had a beginning in order to exist in the present. The same is also true of energy. It might be said that energy can be lumped in with matter in the time-space-matter continuum, because energy is stored in matter.

Take a few moments to study Figure F-1 as you read the next few paragraphs.

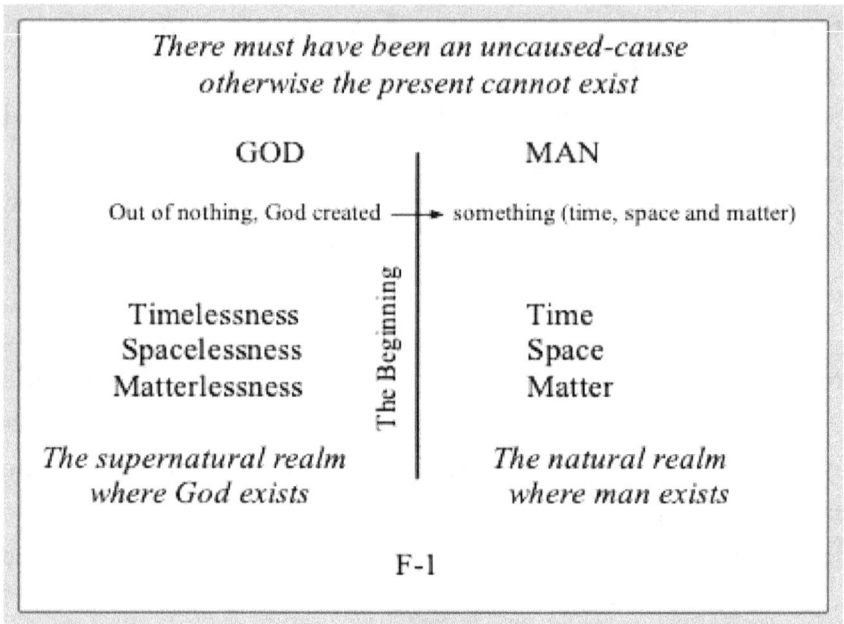

There must have been an uncaused-cause otherwise the present cannot exist

GOD | MAN

Out of nothing, God created ⟶ something (time, space and matter)

The Beginning

Timelessness   Time
Spacelessness   Space
Matterlessness   Matter

The supernatural realm where God exists   *The natural realm where man exists*

F-1

Based on the preceding evidence that time, space, and matter all had to have a beginning, there had to be a timeless-spaceless-matterless state before they began. In F-1 the portion to the right of the beginning might be termed The Natural State in which time, space, and matter exist. The portion to the left of the beginning might be called The Supernatural State, 'super' meaning 'above nature.'

Although man exists in the natural state, only God and other supernatural beings like angels could exist in the supernatural realm. This agrees with the Bible because Scripture teaches that

God and angels are spirits. A spirit does not have flesh and bones and is not bound by time, space, or matter.

In F-1, something (time, space, and matter) comes out of nothing (timelessness, spacelessness, and matterlessness). Interestingly, this is exactly what the Bible teaches: *In the beginning God created the heavens and the earth.* (Genesis 1:1). The word for *create* is the Hebrew word 'bara' (Hebrew is the original language of the Old Testament). It means to create something out of nothing. God said, *Let there be light, and there was light* (Genesis 1:3). He spoke the word, and it was so.

Some people argue, "In order for God to exist, He, too, must have had a beginning." This is faulty reasoning, however, because when the beginning line (Shown in F-1) is crossed from the natural to the supernatural state, human logic and physical laws no longer apply.

Our finite minds cannot completely understand the infinite. The Bible says God's ways are higher than our ways and His thoughts higher than our thoughts (Isaiah 55:8,9).

The preceding argument shows the universe could not have come about by natural means. In order for the universe to exist in the present, it must have been created sometime in the past. If it was created, only a supernatural, all-powerful God could have created it. This is huge evidence for creation and against the theory of cosmic evolution.

2. The Second Law of Thermodynamics

Another evidence that the universe is not eternal is based on the Second Law of Thermodynamics. This law is known as the law of increasing entropy (disorder). The law states, "In a closed system (our universe is a closed system) everything eventually goes to a higher state of disorder (entropy). In other words, things run down and wear out. For example, a cake set on a fence post will eventually disintegrate. A car left out in the weather for 100 years will rust out and fall apart. Our sun, with its limited fuel supply, will eventually burn up.

Put another way, "In a closed, isolated system, the amount of usable energy decreases over time." This means that our universe is running down and will eventually experience heat death, when all the available energy has been converted into unusable energy and dissipates into empty space. The energy will still be there, it just won't be usable.

Another way to understand this is to picture a piece of firewood. Once it is burned in the fireplace, it can't be burned again. The energy is dissipated into the house or out the chimney. If a person has a limited amount of firewood, eventually, all of it will be used up, and he will have nothing left with which to heat his house. So it is with our universe. Once all the useable energy is burned up, our universe will experience heat death.

These facts prove the universe cannot be eternal. If it was, the stars would have already burned out since they have a limited amount of fuel. Since the stars haven't yet burned out, they can't be infinitely old.

In an attempt to show the universe is eternal and to overcome the Second Law of Thermodynamics, Fred Hoyle, proposed what is known as the Steady-State Theory. The theory proposes that hydrogen atoms are coming into existence in deep space keeping the universe from running down. But there is one huge problem with this theory. It goes against the Principle of Causality. Hydrogen atoms cannot come out of nothing; they have to come from somewhere. This brings the argument full circle – only a supernatural God who transcends the laws of nature could have brought things into existence.[8]

Without God, a person is faced with something (time, space, matter, energy, hydrogen atoms, the universe, etc.) coming out of nothing. This simply can't happen.

3. What about the big bang theory?

Many cosmic evolutionists also believe there was a time when the matter in the universe was clumped together and blew up in a "big bang" causing the myriad of galaxies we see today. One reason they believe this is because it appears the galaxies are expanding outward from a central point. There also seems to be an energy echo in the universe as if there was a huge explosion sometime in the past.

Is it possible that God used a "big bang" to create the universe? It is possible, but it must be understood He also would have had to create the matter for the big bang. A clump of matter doesn't just show up. It has to come from somewhere. In addition, God would have had to create the empty space in which to place the clump of matter.[9]

Rather than postulating a big bang, it seems more reasonable to accept the Bible at face value. It simply states that God created everything out of nothing (Genesis 1:1), which agrees completely with the physical Principle of Causality. Amazingly, the Bible also states that God spoke things into existence. For example, God said, "Let the earth sprout vegetation...and it was so." (Genesis 1:11) .

An all-powerful God living in a supernatural realm has the power to create a material universe in a natural realm. Nothing is

8. Henry M. Morris, *Scientific Creationism,* (Mater Books, 1985), 26.

9. Geisler, 102-106

beyond His ability. The only thing God cannot do is to violate His own character. For example, since God is completely holy, He cannot lie. This gives us another reason to believe what He says in the Bible is true.

Once everything was created, creationists believe God set in motion all of the other laws like the laws of thermodynamics. The fact there are so many perfect laws (gravity, centrifugal force, the laws of thermodynamics, etc.) that govern the physical universe goes completely against the idea of evolution, which is based on the premise of random, non-intelligence. Everything in the universe screams that an awesome intelligence, far greater than man, created it all. That intelligence is God.

4. What about the rebound theory?

Some cosmic evolutionists believe in a rebound theory stating the universe has been expanding and collapsing on itself over eons of time. The theory also assumes the eternal nature of matter. Again, this violates the Principle of Causality because the initial matter for the universe had to come from somewhere. The rebound theory also violates the Second Law of Thermodynamics. If the universe were contracting and expanding, it would, like a bouncing ball, eventually slow down and stop bouncing. If it were infinitely old, it would have run down and stopped by now. Since it hasn't, it can't be eternal. Since it isn't eternal, it had to have come into existence sometime in the past. Christians call this event, creation.[10]

. . .

---

10. Geisler, 232

5. Summary regarding cosmic evolution

In summary, based on the laws of science, the universe can't be infinitely old. If it is not infinitely old, then it came into existence sometime in the past. When it came into existence in the past, it had to come out of nothing. If it came out of nothing, it had to be created. If it was created, the only logical explanation is that God created it. Simple logic says that something coming out of nothing is a supernatural event. Supernatural events necessitate a supernatural source. Creationists call that supernatural source, God.

It has been rightly said that believing in cosmic evolution takes more faith than believing in creation. Simply put, not only is there no compelling evidence for cosmic evolution, there is strong evidence against it. Conversely, all the evidence against cosmic evolution points toward special creation.

IS CHEMICAL EVOLUTION TRUE?

Chemical evolution is the belief that first-life on earth developed by natural means. Does the evidence support this theory? Decide for yourself.

1. The primordial pond?

Evolutionary scientists believe life developed in a primordial pond sometime after the earth was formed and cooled. They base their belief partly on the experiments of Harold Urey and Stanley Miller who attempted to duplicate what they thought the earth's early atmosphere might have been like. They set up experiments where they passed an electrical discharge (simulating lightning) through various gases (hydrogen, nitrogen, ammonia, and carbon dioxide), simulating earth's early atmosphere. Their experiments showed that amino acids (the basic building blocks of life) could be formed in this way.[11]

Their initial success sent euphoria through the evolutionist community. People made claims they were on the brink of creating life in the laboratory. Based on all the hype, many people concluded they had created life. For many folks, these experiments made evolution an open-and-shut case. Man had finally shown how first-life had come about by totally natural means. This, however, was and still is a gross misunderstanding of what really happened. Even though Urey and Miller did create some basic amino acids, they never created life itself, or anything close to it. The amino acids never developed further into the things necessary for real life – proteins, DNA chains, or cells. Although the experiments created a stir, those who know the whole story realize the experiments proved essentially nothing in regard to how life could have come about by natural means. Similar experiments have shown no greater success either.

It is rarely mentioned that the experiments of Urey and Miller went way beyond what could have taken place in nature. In essence the scientists pulled out all the stops. On the one hand, they said they were trying to create life through totally natural means. On the other hand, they manipulated materials in ways that do not mirror nature. For example, they used concentrations of gases not found anywhere on earth. They also left out oxygen because they knew it would destroy the process they were trying to create. Now, scientists believe oxygen was present in earth's early atmosphere. This fact alone invalidates any findings of these experiments. The scientists also left out sunlight because they knew cosmic radiation would undermine their results. In short, instead of using natural

---

11. Phillip Johnson, *Darwin on Trial*, (Intervarsity Press, 1993), 104,105.

means, these scientists injected as much intelligence as humanly possible. Even so, the experiments failed.[12]

In all probability, the primordial pond proposed by these and other scientists never existed, and even if it did, it offers only dead ends in the search for any natural explanation for first-life.

2. Is it possible to get life from non-life?

There are also a number of other reasons why chemical evolution is an invalid theory. For example, it has never been shown anywhere on earth that life can spontaneously arise from non-life, but that is precisely what the theory of evolution postulates.

There was a time when most people accepted the theory of Spontaneous Generation. They believed that flies, worms, and mice could develop directly from nonliving matter like mud and decaying flesh. In 1668, Francesco Redi proved this idea to be false when he demonstrated that maggots did not appear on meat if other flies were kept away. Louis Pasteur (1822-1895) later showed that microorganisms would grow in sterilized broth only if the broth was first exposed to air that contained spores (reproductive cells).

It is rather astonishing that many scientists today, by believing in chemical evolution (that first-life came from non-life) are, in essence, supporting a modern form of spontaneous generation.

In addition, evolutionists have never been able to show any non-living mechanism that can select amino acids, sort them, and build genes to form even a single living cell. Only previous living material containing the code of life (DNA) can beget new living material. This previously living material has built-in intelligence. Life demands intelligence, not a non-directed process like evolution.

---

12. Geisler, 227.

Even with all the roadblocks, evolutionists continue to speculate how life might have come from non-life. They have proposed such theories as the "RNA first" and "protein first" hypotheses, but all have proved inadequate.

Evolutionists know that in contemporary living organisms – DNA, RNA, and proteins are mutually dependent, but these same scientists are at a total loss as to how something as complex as a DNA strand could have developed by natural means. Amazingly, even one strand of DNA has as much information as a volume of the Encyclopedia Britannica, and it is all perfectly coded.

> The simplest organism capable of independent life, the prokaryote bacterial cell, is a masterpiece of miniaturized complexity, which makes a spaceship seem rather low-tech. Even if one assumes that something much simpler than a bacterial cell might suffice to start Darwinist evolution on its way – a DNA or RNA macromolecule, for example – the possibility that such a complex entity could assemble itself by chance is still fantastically unlikely, even if billions of years had been available.[13]

In the last several years, scientists have attempted to bypass experimental difficulties using computer simulations, but these, too, have resulted in no real progress in finding any natural origin of first-life.

> A general review of prebiological evolutionary theories in 1988 by Klaus Dose concluded that "At present, all discussions on principal theories and experiments in the field either end in stalemate or in a confession of ignorance."

---

13. Johnson, 105,106.

Gerald Joyce's 1989 review article ended with the somber observation that origin of life researchers have grown accustomed to a "lack of relevant experimental data" and a high level of frustration.[14]

The possibility of life coming together by chance is so incredibly small that Fred Hoyle, who seemingly changed from being an evolutionist to a creationist, said it would be the same odds as a tornado sweeping through a junkyard and assembling a fully functional Boeing 747 from the parts therein.[15]

Biologist, Dr. Edwin Conklin, said, "The probability of life originating from accident is comparable to the probability of the unabridged dictionary resulting from an explosion in a printing shop."[16]

When faced with lack of evidence, and the statistical impossibility of chemical evolution, evolutionists often rely on philosophical arguments and rhetoric like,

Life obviously exists, and if a naturalistic process is the only conceivable explanation for its existence, then the difficulties must not be as insuperable as they appear... or... life seems to have existed in cellular form nearly four billion years ago, perhaps as soon as the earth had sufficiently cooled. That means that the emergence of the first self-replicating molecules and the subsequent evolution of all the machinery of the cell had to occur within a brief period of geological time... the spontaneous origin of life must be relatively easy since it happened so quickly on the early

---

14. Ibid., p. 109.
15. Ibid., p. 106.
16. Blick., p. 16.

earth... or... (the anthropic principle) if the circumstances required for life to evolve had not existed we would not be here to comment upon the matter. Those circumstances may seem very unlikely given our limited knowledge, but we have no way of knowing how many universes there are or may have been. In an infinity of time and space even the most unlikely event must happen at least once...[17]

Die-hard evolutionists like Richard Dawkins who realize they have no real evidence for their theory, try to turn the tide by saying the lack of evidence is actually a plus. In other words, if evolutionists could somehow reproduce life from non-life that would prove just how easy evolution is. Since it is obviously quite complicated, one would expect that scientists couldn't easily duplicate it in the laboratory. In this regard, Dawkins said,

An apparently miraculous theory is exactly the kind of theory we should be looking for in this particular matter of the origin of life... because evolution has equipped our brains with a subjective consciousness of risk and improbability suitable for creatures with a lifetime of less than one century."[18]

When people like Richard Dawkins start using fanciful arguments, it is clear that evolutionists have little, if any evidence to support their position. If they did have credible evidence, they would shout it from the rooftops.

If evolutionists agree they should be looking for a miraculous

---

17. Johnson., p. 106.
18. Ibid., p. 107.

theory, why don't they look to God? The reason is clear – many don't want to.

Physiologist, Dr. T. N. Tahmisian from the U.S. Atomic Energy Commission said, "Scientists who go about teaching that evolution is a fact are great con men, and the story they are telling may be the greatest hoax ever. In explaining evolution we do not have one iota of fact."[19]

From everything humans know, the only one who could make life out of non-life is an intelligent, all-powerful, all-knowing God.

Simply stated, there is no compelling support for chemical evolution, but there is considerable evidence to refute it. And the evidence against it is powerful evidence for creation; because, if evolution is false, the only other option is creation.

IS BIOLOGICAL EVOLUTION TRUE?

Biological evolution is the belief that all existing species of plants and animals have developed from previously existing species through a gradual process known as natural selection.

Before we consider the evidence, let's first gain a basic understanding of the theory of biological evolution as set forth by Charles Darwin.

1. Charles Darwin and the theory of biological evolution

Charles Robert Darwin was born in England in 1809. Although he studied medicine, the only educational degree he received was in theology from Cambridge University in 1831. He was the grandson of Erasmus Darwin, who himself, had proposed a theory of evolution in the 1790s.

---

19. Blick., p. 16

From 1831 to 1836 Charles Darwin served as a British Naturalist on board the H.M.S. Beagle as it sailed from England with the mission of surveying the shores of Chile, Peru, and some islands in the Pacific, as well as carrying a chain of chronometrical measurements around the world. Part of the cruise was spent in the Galapagos Islands, an archipelago of thirteen small volcanic islands on the equator about 600 miles off the coast of South America.

While on those islands, Darwin noticed variations in finches, lizards, and turtles. The finches on the different islands had variations in size, plumage, beak shape, and behavior. Darwin surmised that these variations were caused by a process of change he called natural selection which aided the various finches in some way. Different beak shapes aided in eating different foods. Some were for probing flowers while others were for boring into wood. Different colors allowed the various finches to blend into their surroundings thus increasing their chances of survival.

From these and other observations, Darwin returned to England and eventually published his book "On the Origin of Species by Means of Natural Selection, or the Preservation of Favoured Races in the Struggle for Life" in 1859.

Although Charles Darwin was not the first person to propose an evolutionary theory, he was the first to show a mechanism by which it could take place.

Darwin showed that living things commonly produce many more offspring than are necessary to replace themselves. The earth cannot possibly support all these organisms, and so they must compete for such necessities as food and shelter. Their lives are also threatened by animals that prey on them, by unfavorable weather, and by other environmental conditions. Darwin suggested that some members of a species have traits that aid them in this struggle for life. Other members have less favorable traits and, therefore, are less likely to survive or reproduce. On average, the members with favorable traits live longer and produce more offspring than do the others. They also pass on the favorable traits to their young. The unfavorable traits are eventually eliminated. When this process occurs in two isolated populations of one species, members of one species may become so genetically different that they will be regarded as separate species.[20]

In summary, Darwin's theory had three important premises. First, organisms varied. Second, these variations could be inherited. Third, all organisms were subject to an intense struggle for survival which favored those with positive variations.

To illustrate how Darwin's theory differed from previous theories, consider the following. The Frenchman Lamark had a theory supporting the idea that giraffes got longer necks by stretching them to get higher leaves. The stretching caused inner forces in the giraffe to pass the characteristic longer necks on to their offspring. Although this sounded good, Lamark never could define what kind of inner forces were involved.

Darwinian evolution, on the other hand, would say some giraffes are born with slightly longer necks because, in every species, there are variations. The giraffes with longer necks would have a greater capacity to survive because they could reach leaves on higher tree branches during times of food scarcity. They would thus be more likely to survive and reproduce offspring with this same advantage or even greater advantages.

This process of natural selection, later called 'the survival of the

---

20. 1991 *World Book Multimedia Encyclopedia* Article on Charles Darwin

fittest,' was the first time a logical and totally natural theory for evolution had been set forth.

Although the theory could not be proved and initially caused heated debate, scientists eventually accepted it, and evolution permeated the fabric of society.

The question arises, however, "Does the evidence really support the theory of biological evolution?" To answer this question, let's take a closer look.

2. The difference between micro and macroevolution

Within the context of biology there are supposedly two types of evolution: microevolution and macroevolution. Micro means very small. Macro means very large.

Microevolution involves changes within one kind of plant or animal. For example, cows can be bred to produce varying characteristics of color, size, milk production, etc. Flowers can be raised to get different colors... Not only can things be purposely bred to produce change, but God has programmed the ability to change within every creature or plant in order to help it adapt to its environment. Even after these changes take place, it is important to note that cattle are still cattle, and flowers are still flowers.

Macroevolution, on the other hand, purports that one kind of plant or animal can change into another kind if given enough time. If cattle are bred long enough they might gradually change into horses, for example. Simply stated, there is a huge problem with macroevolution; not only has no one seen it happen, there is no credible evidence that it has ever happened.

What Darwin discovered in the Galapagos Islands was nothing more than microevolution, which is better called hybridization. In other words, in the genetic makeup of all animals (finches included) is the capacity for change. When finches breed, especially in isolated areas like the various islands in the Galapagos chain, the results can be amazing. They will adapt to their environment. Such breeding can produce big finches, small finches, finches with various-sized beaks, and various colors of plumage, but those finches will never become hawks. There is a limit to the change that can take place in each kind of plant or animal.

One classic example that evolutionists tried to use to support their theory is the peppered moth. Peppered moths have both white and black on their wings. When the predominantly white moths began to disappear in an area of England and the predominantly black moths thrived, scientists said, "Hurrah! Clear evidence of evolution." They believed the moths were adapting to their environment. Later the real reason for the change became apparent. The towns where this was happening were coal-burning towns. Soot accumulation on the trees made the predominantly white moths much easier targets for birds. The darker moths blended in and thus survived. In towns that switched from coal to other fuels, the predominantly white moths reappeared. This was not a case of evolutionary change but of birds spotting contrasting colors. Unfortunately, there are still publications that teach the peppered moth story as clear evidence for evolution. The 1997 World Book Multimedia Encyclopedia is one of them.

Evolutionists say it is possible to get whole new species by cross-breeding. They define a species as a group of animals that can effectively breed with each other. Although it is possible to cross-breed pigeons so the pigeons at either end of the spectrum can no longer effectively breed (and are thus categorized by evolutionists as different species), they still have similar characteristics and are part of the pigeon kind. They never become anything more or less than pigeons.

Today, when people refer to biological evolution, they are almost always referring to macroevolution. They believe the various array of plants and animals alive today somehow evolved from the first-life form. In essence they claim we have gone from microbe to man through a gradual process of change. Although this sounds plausible, there is not one shred of evidence to support macroevolution. Evolutionists will argue that change happens so slowly we can't see it, but the fact is, there is no evidence to support such changes ever happened at all.

No one debates that hybridization takes place (microevolution). God programmed into all creatures the ability to change within certain limits. Creationists, however, strongly oppose the notion of macroevolution, because no one has ever seen it happen in the past or present. It is strictly conjecture.

The Bible even says everything God created reproduces after its own kind. For example, Genesis 1:24-25 states, *Then God said, "Let the earth bring forth living creatures after their kind: cattle and creeping things and beasts of the earth after their kind;" and it was so. And God made the beasts of the earth after their kind, and the cattle after their kind, and everything that creeps on the ground after its kind; and God saw that it was good.*

Creationists believe that God created all the various kinds of animals and that those animals have been reproducing after their kind ever since. This is precisely what we see in the real world. Macroevolution, on the other hand, has no support and is nothing more than wishful thinking.

3. Evidence from the fossil record

If macroevolution were true, the place to find any real evidence would be in the fossil record. If indeed we have gone from microbe to man, as evolutionists claim, the fossil record should be pregnant with intermediate species between all of the different kinds of plants and animals we see today. The simple truth is, the intermediate species are not there. The missing links have remained missing. Even the so-called missing links between ape and man have never been conclusively shown to be anything more than either fully human or fully ape. Creationists believe the missing links will remain missing because they never existed.

Darwin himself recognized the problem in the fossil record. He said, "Why is not every geological formation and every stratum full of such intermediate links? Geology assuredly does not reveal any such finely graduated organic chain, and this perhaps, is the most obvious and gravest objection which can be urged against my theory."[21]

Darwin hoped the area of paleontology (the study of fossils) would provide support for his theory in the years following the initial publication of his book. It has now been more than 160 years since Darwin's book was first published, and the support for evolution in the fossil record has only gotten worse. No truly intermediate species have been found. Even Stephen Jay Gould, the noted Harvard paleontologist who is an ardent evolutionist, had to admit,

> The extreme rarity of transitional forms in the fossil record persists as the trade secret of paleontology. The evolutionary trees that adorn our textbooks have data only at the tops and nodes of their branches; the rest is inference, however reasonable, not the evidence of fossils.[22]

Some evolutionists will argue that archaeopteryx is a transitional form between bird and reptile, but in more recent days it has been shown that archaeopteryx had normal flight feathers

21. Charles Darwin, *The Origin of Species*, p. 280.
22. Stephen Jay Gould, *"Evolution's Erratic Pace."* Natural History, 1977, p. 14.

and was nothing more than a bird. Other supposed transitional forms have all essentially led to the same dead end. The amazing thing is, if macroevolution was true, the fossil record would be full of such forms, but it is not.

If the fossil record does not have transitional forms, what does it show? It shows that species do not arise gradually, but all at once and fully formed. This is exactly what the theory of creation predicts.

The fossil record also shows stasis, which means species appear in the fossil record looking much the same as when they disappeared. Any changes are limited and directionless. In other words we don't see any species moving up an evolutionary ladder.

Evolutionists argue that the deepest rock layers (and thus the oldest) contain fossils of simple creatures, while the most shallow rock layers (and thus the youngest) contain the more complex creatures. They say this is what evolution predicts. The fact is, there are areas where the simplest fossils are closer to the surface and the more advanced fossils in deeper strata, contradicting the evolutionary model.

Creationists say a large part of the fossil record is a result of the Biblical flood. The areas where the simple fossils are deeper in the strata are evidence of a sifting action that occurred as dead creatures settled to the bottom of water-filled areas. The larger creatures were able to survive and fight for life longer than the smaller, simpler creatures and thus are closer to the top.

Because the evidence in the fossil record does not support macroevolution, some evolutionists have proposed such theories as Punctuated Equilibrium. Punctuated equilibrium postulates that there were sudden catastrophic jumps in the fossil record followed by long periods of stability.

The problem with such theories is there is no evidence to

support them. On the contrary, Darwin admitted that the suddenness in the fossil record was evidence in favor of creation.

Such theories as punctuated equilibrium almost sound like creationism. Perhaps some evolutionists don't realize what they are saying.

4. Evidence from mutations

Evolutionists say mutations help account for biological evolution. They believe if a mutation gives a creature some kind of advantage it will aid in the creature's survival and be passed on to the next generation.

Although mutations do occur, there are two insurmountable difficulties associated with the mutation theory. The first is all actually observed mutations fit into the category of micro-mutations. In other words they are relatively small and insignificant. An accumulation of millions of mutations would be necessary to change one basic kind into another or to develop a major organ.

A second grave difficulty is that practically all observed mutations are harmful and usually fatal to the creature experiencing them. Beneficial mutations are so rare and questionable, their existence is still in doubt.[23]

In regard to mutations, consider the possible formation of a human eye. An eye needs a lens, muscles, retina, optic nerve, cones, cornea, blood supply, eyelid, eyelashes, depth perception (two eyes are needed for this), and tear ducts. This would take literally millions, if not billions, of small mutations, each one having to be passed on to the next generation. Also, a center in the brain would

---

23. Henry M. Morris, *Evolution and the Modern Christian* (Baker Book House, 1967), 27,28.

need to develop to interpret the information received through the optic nerve and make sense of it, integrating it into the motor function of the body. Considering that 99.9 percent of mutations are negative, the statistical possibility of forming something as complex as an eye is essentially zero. In addition, until an eye is fully formed, it is of no advantage to the creature that possesses it. In fact, it would be a hindrance and lessen a creature's chance of survival. This totally undermines the idea of natural selection and macroevolution.

To overcome the problem of micro-mutations, some evolutionists have postulated macro-mutations. A macro-mutation would be an eye suddenly appearing, fully functional. This is beyond the realm of reason. Macro-mutations have never been observed experimentally or in the natural world. In addition, there is no known mechanism that could ever make them occur.[24] The only one who could perform such a feat is God.

Some evolutionists point to such things as penicillin-resistant bacteria or pesticide-resistant insects as examples of effective evolution. At best, these are examples of micro-mutations and support microevolution – change within a kind.

Mutations provide no compelling evidence for the theory of macroevolution, but rather strong evidence against it.

5. Evidence from genetics and complexity

One of the greatest problems for evolutionists, besides the missing links in the fossil record, is the problem of explaining the origin of complex new systems. Every living creature has its own extremely complex genetic code. The code for a man is different than that of an ape. The code for a horse is different than that of a

24. Ibid. p. 29.

cow. Not only are these codes unbelievably complex, they are perfect.

> Not only was the first living cell exceedingly complex, but higher forms of life are even more complex. If the genetic information in a one-cell animal exceeds that in a volume of the Encyclopedia Britannica, the information in the human brain is greater than that in the Library of Congress. If it takes an intelligent cause to produce the simple first life form, no less is needed for human life.[25]

To think that something as complex as the genetic code could happen by gradual processes is like trying to change the sentence, "She likes ice cream," into the book "War and Peace," one letter at a time, each change taking a generation. The first change might be "She likes mice cream." The second change might be "She likes mice scream." The third change might be "Shed likes mice scream." Subsequent changes might yield "Shedl. Zlikes: bmicet xscrheaml." Obviously not only do changes change the meaning of the sentence, but after several changes, the words become nonsense. In the case of living things, nonsense means extinction. The book "War and Peace" could never be produced this way by random chance, no matter how much time was given. In the same way, the genetic code of even the simplest creature could never change into the code of another creature randomly.

In more mundane terms, consider the human body. It has a circulatory system, digestive system, nervous system, immune system, reproductive system, respiratory system, heating and cooling system, balance system... brain, heart, eyes, sense of smell, touch, hearing, hormones, skin, and speech, to name a few. All work

---

25. Norman L. Geisler, p. 227

in amazing harmony. Indeed, we do not realize how incredibly complex our bodies are until something goes wrong. For anyone to believe this intricate myriad of interrelated complex systems evolved requires much more faith than believing in God.

In addition, the fact that creatures appear in the fossil record suddenly and fully formed with these immense genetic codes in perfect working order is strong evidence for creation.

6. Evidence from vestigial organs

Evolutionists claim that such organs as the human appendix, ear muscles, and the third eyelid are vestiges of the past. In other words they were useful during some previous evolutionary age but not now. The problem with this line of reasoning is that the list of over 100 of these organs (when the idea was first proposed) has shrunk to about a half dozen today. For example, the endocrine glands, which were once thought to be vestigial, are now known to help with the production of hormones. As scientific thought advances, more and more uses become apparent.

Just because a use is not known for a particular organ does not mean one does not exist. And just because organs can be removed without apparent harm to the body does not mean they had no function. Other organs may compensate once certain other organs are gone.[26]

In reality, if any organs in humans or other creatures are truly vestigial, it would not show the advance of evolution but the decline from a perfect creation. Vestigial organs would mean we had organs that once had a purpose but now no longer function according to a perfect original design.

. . .

26. Ibid., p. 21

7. Evidence from systemic change

Macroevolution requires large-scale change as one type of organism evolves into another. Macroevolution also says it happens over a long period of time. This, however, is impossible when the need for simultaneous change is seen. For example,

> One can make small changes in a car gradually over a period of time, without changing its basic type. One can change the shape of the fenders, its color, and its trim gradually. But if a change is in the size of the pistons, this will involve simultaneous changes in the camshaft, block, and cooling system. Otherwise, the new engine will not function. Likewise, changing from a fish to a reptile or a reptile to a bird, calls for major changes throughout the system of the animal. All these changes must occur simultaneously, or blood oxygenation will not go with the lung development, will not match nasal passage and throat changes, autonomic breathing reflexes in the brain, thoracic musculature and membranes. Gradual evolution cannot account for this.[27]

There is no way the theory of macroevolution can account for systemic changes in any creature.

8. Other circumstantial evidences

Evolutionists have said the following are also evidence for evolution:

- **Classification** – It is possible to arrange the various

---

27. Ibid., p. 228.

kinds of plants and animals into categories of species, genera, families, orders, etc.

- **Comparative Anatomy** – There are similarities in skeletal structure, such as between apes and men, or horses and elephants.
- **Embryology** – There are similarities in embryos of different kinds of animals.
- **Biochemistry** – All living organisms are composed of certain basic chemical substances such as amino acids, proteins, DNA, etc.
- **Physiology** – There are similarities in things like blood precipitates and behavior characteristics.

It is a simple fact that all of the above-mentioned areas support the theory of creation as well as evolution. If God created everything, it would seem logical that His creation could be classified. If creatures needed to walk or run, it makes sense that God would give them legs. It is reasonable to conclude that the embryology, biochemistry and physiology of certain animals would also be closely connected. None of these supposed evidences for evolution add any credibility to the theory.

9. What about theistic evolution?

Because some Christians don't know the true evidence against evolution, they have postulated that God used evolution as His means of creating the world. This idea has at least four major flaws.

First, Romans 5:12 clearly states there was no death before the sin of man entered the world. The whole process of evolution involves struggle and death over millions of years, long before organisms could have evolved into man. If evolution is correct, then death is not the result of sin, and there is no need for a Savior. This totally goes against the teaching of Scripture.

Second, theistic evolution postulates a completely random, non-directed, natural process. Since God is an intelligent creature, theistic evolution is a contradiction in terms. It would mean that God, the epitome of intelligence, used evolution, the epitome of non-directed ignorance. Theism and evolution don't mix.

The third reason why theistic evolution is flawed is because it goes completely contrary to God's nature. It is inconceivable that a loving God would use such an inefficient, gruesome method as macroevolution for creating new life forms. Evolution involves struggle and death over millions of years. In addition, racism, abortion, Naziism, euthanasia, and other evils are supported by evolutionary thinking. If man evolved, there is no ultimate right or wrong. Why not get rid of unwanted babies, old people, and other less-than-desirable people groups? That is precisely what Hitler and other evolutionists have tried to do.

There is no way a loving God would utilize a system like evolution to accomplish His plans.

The fourth major flaw in theistic evolution is found in Genesis 1:1, which states, *In the beginning, God created the heavens and the earth.* The Hebrew word for create is 'bara.' It means to create something out of nothing. Creating something out of nothing is supernatural. Evolution, on the other hand, is naturalistic.

If cosmic and chemical evolution are false, the logical conclusion is that any form of evolution is false, including theistic evolution. God did not need a process like evolution to do anything. God spoke things into existence, and this is what logic and evidence indicate actually happened.

. . .

10. Evidence from the created world

Perhaps one of the greatest evidences for creation is the world around us. Romans 1:20 states, *For since the creation of the world His (God's) invisible attributes, His eternal power and divine nature, have been clearly seen, being understood through what has been made, so that they are without excuse.* Simply stated, people who look at the world around them and still reject God, will be without excuse when they stand before Him at judgment. God says His created world is enough to make anyone believe.

The birth of a baby, and its change from living in a water environment to living in an air environment – the changing of a caterpillar into a butterfly – the migratory habits of birds – the love of two people for each other – the emotions of joy and sorrow – and a thousand other things not explained by evolution, should be enough to make a person wake up and say, "Wow, God created it all!"

CONCLUDING REMARKS

King David was correct when he said in Psalm 139:14, *I will give thanks to Thee, for I am fearfully and wonderfully made; wonderful are Thy works, and my soul knows it very well.*

The verdict is in. The evidence for evolution simply is not there – not for cosmic evolution, chemical evolution, biological evolution, or theistic evolution.

Dr. Louis Bounoure, Director of Research at the National Center of Scientific Research in France, said, "Evolutionism is a fairy tale for grown-ups. This theory has helped nothing in the progress of science. It is useless."[28]

On the other hand, all the evidence indicates that an incredible

---

28. Blick, p. 17.

intelligence, far above man, created the universe and everything in it. His name is God. And the great news is, He wants to have a personal relationship with you and me through His Son, Jesus Christ, who died for our sins and rose from the dead. All we need to do is to put our faith in Him. Now that's amazing!

DISCUSSION QUESTIONS

HAS SCIENCE DISPROVED THE BIBLE? IS EVOLUTION TRUE?

1. How has this study affected your view of Science and the Bible?

2. How has this study affected your view of the theory of evolution?

3. What are some of the scientific things in the Bible that indicate it is scientifically accurate?

4. What is the difference between cosmic, chemical, and biological evolution?

5. What evidence against the theory of evolution stood out most in your mind?

6. What evidence for creation stood out most in your mind?

7. What is the difference between micro and macroevolution?

8. Briefly summarize the evidence against biological evolution in the following areas:

    - the fossil record

    - mutations

    - genetics and complexity

- vestigial organs

- systemic change

- circumstantial evidences

- the created world

9. Why is theistic evolution a contradiction?

SEVEN

HOW IS CHRISTIANITY DIFFERENT FROM OTHER RELIGIONS?

S ome people believe all religions are pretty much the same. After all, religions believe in some sort of deity or higher power, usually involve some form of worship, and promote doing good deeds. Even though this is generally true, there are some major differences between Christianity and other religions. In order to understand the unique nature of Christianity, it is helpful to look at the five major world religions, some modern religions, and various cults.

Much of the following information was gleaned from the Rose Publishing pamphlet entitled Christianity, Cults and Religions distributed by Rose Publishing. Other books that were also helpful were So What's the Difference by Fritz Ridenour and Kingdom of the Cults by Walter Martin.

1. Biblical Christianity

Christianity was founded by Jesus Christ approximately AD 30-

33 in the Judean province of Palestine.[1] Christians follow the teachings of the Bible that they believe is God's inspired Word. They also believe Jesus is God's Son, part of the Trinity of Father, Son, and Holy Spirit. In addition, they believe Jesus came to die for the sins of the world. Christians claim Jesus rose from the dead on the third day after He was crucified. Even though all people have a sin nature (a natural bent toward sinning), each person can be saved by placing his or her faith in God. It is God's grace (God's unmerited favor), not good works that saves a person. A person must believe in his heart that Jesus died for his sins and physically rose from the dead. Believing in Jesus involves more than one's intellect; it means making a personal commitment to follow Christ in daily life. This means living by biblical principles and obeying the inner promptings of the Holy Spirit, Who indwells Christians at the moment of salvation. When a person places his faith in Christ in this way, he is saved. People who are truly saved cannot lose their salvation. At the moment of physical death, the spirit of a saved person goes directly into God's presence. One day, the physical bodies of Christians will be resurrected, even if they have decomposed or have been cremated. These bodies will be changed into immortal, glorified bodies, be reunited with their spirits, and spend eternity with God in Heaven.

2. Buddhism

Buddhism was founded by Buddha (Siddhartha Gautama) in India in about 525 BC. Buddhism is an offshoot of Hinduism. It follows the teachings found in the Tripitaka (Three Baskets) that has more than 100 volumes. Buddhists do not believe a person has a soul or spirit. They also do not believe in heaven or hell. A person's

---

1. *Christianity, Cults and Religions,*)Rose Publishing, 2000), 2.

feelings and desires may be reincarnated into another person. The goal of life, according to Buddhists, is Nirvana, to eliminate all desires or cravings and, in this way, be able to escape suffering. The Eightfold Path is a system to free Buddhists from desiring anything.[2] The Eightfold Path includes right viewpoint, right aspiration, right speech, right behavior, right occupation, right effort, right mindfulness, and right meditation. Buddha promised that all who follow this path would reach Nirvana.[3]

3. Hinduism

Hinduism has no single founder. It has many sects and began around 1800-1000 BC in India. Hindus follow the teachings found in the Vedas (oldest writings from about 1000 BC), the Upanishads, and the Bhagavad-Gita. After a person dies, Hindus believe he is reincarnated into a better status (good karma) if the person has behaved well. If not, he can be reborn and pay for past sins (bad karma) by suffering. Hindus believe that salvation is the release from the cycles of reincarnation. This is achieved through Yoga and meditation. The process can take many lifetimes. Final salvation is absorption or union with Brahman, the Hindu creator god.[4]

4. Islam

The man Muhammad founded Islam about AD 610 in Mecca and Medina. The current headquarters is in Mecca, Saudi Arabia. Islam's main sects are Sunni and Shi'ite. Muslims (followers of Islam) follow the teachings of the Qur'an (Koran) and the Hadith

---

2. Ibid., p. 10.
3. Fritz Ridenour, *So What's the Difference* (Regal Books, 1979), 86.
4. *Christianity, Cults and Religions*, p. 8.

(their tradition). They believe their god, Allah, sent Muhammad into the world as his prophet with the true teachings so that Islam could rule the world. Islam is more than a religion; it is a culture that controls every aspect of life (religious, political, economic, social, etc.) in Islamic countries. According to Islam, there are two groups of people in the world: "the house of Islam," made up of those who follow Islamic teachings, and "the house of war" made up of everyone else. It is up to Muslims to fight against the rest of the world (those in the house of war), until they are brought into submission to Allah. Muslims believe that humans are basically good but fallible and in need of guidance. The balance between good and bad deeds determines eternal destiny in paradise or hell. God's mercy may tip the balance, but it is arbitrary and uncertain. Muslims believe that if a person dies in battle for the cause of Allah, his soul goes directly to paradise. Muslims believe in the resurrection of the body and a final judgment. Those who believe in Islam will receive eternal rewards. Those who reject Islam (infidels) will suffer eternally in hell.[5]

5. Judaism

Judaism's founder is Abraham. The religion began in approximately 2000 BC in the Middle East. Jews follow the Tanakh (Old Testament), especially the Torah (the first 5 books of the Old Testament) and the Talmud (explanation of the Tanakh). Some Jews believe that prayer, repentance, and obeying the Law are necessary for salvation. Others believe that salvation is the improvement of society. Some Jews also believe there will be a physical resurrection. The obedient will live forever with God, and

---

5. Ibid., p. 11.

the unrighteous will suffer. Some Jews do not believe in a conscious life after death.[6]

MODERN RELIGIONS AND CULTS – BRIEF SUMMARIES

1. Baha'i World Faith

Baha'i was founded by Mizra Ali Muhammed (the Bab) and Mizra Husayn Ali (Baha'u'llah) in 1844 in Iran. The current headquarters is in Haifa, Israel. Those in the Baha'i faith follow the writings of Baha'u'llah and Abdu'l-Baha, known as the Kitab-i-Aqdas and Kitab-i-lqan. They also follow the Bible as spiritually interpreted to conform to Baha'i theology. Those who follow Baha'i believe salvation comes from faith in the manifestation of God (Baha'u'llah) and knowing and living by Baha'u'llah's principles and teachings. Personal immortality is based on good works, with rewards for the faithful. Heaven and hell are conditions, not places. To those in the Baha'i faith, Jesus is just one of many manifestations of God. Each manifestation supersedes the previous, giving new teachings. Jesus, who superseded Moses, was superseded by Muhammad, and most recently by the greatest manifestation, Baha'u'llah, who supposedly is Jesus returned to earth.[7]

2. Christian Science

Christian Science was founded in 1875 by Mary Baker Eddy in Massachusetts, which is the current headquarters. Christian Scientists follow the book Science and Health, With Key to the Scriptures written by Mrs. Eddy. They also follow other miscellaneous writings. Christian Scientists see the Bible as

---

6. Ibid., p. 8.
7. Ibid., p. 11.

unreliable when compared with Mrs. Eddy's writings. According to Christian Science, humanity is already eternally saved. Sin, evil, sickness, and death are not real, and heaven and hell are just states of mind. The way to reach heaven is by attaining harmony (oneness with God).[8]

3. Hare Krishna

This religion was founded in 1965 in New York by Bhaktivedanta Swami Prabhupada. It is based on Hindu teachings from the AD 1500s. Those who follow Hare Krishna believe constantly chanting Krishna's name, having total devotion to Krishna, worshipping images, and obeying the rules of ISKCON (International Society for Krishna Consciousness) throughout many reincarnated lives releases a follower from bad karma. Those who are unenlightened continue in endless reincarnation (rebirth on earth) based on the sinful acts of their previous lives.[9]

4. Jehovah's Witnesses

The Jehovah's Witness religion was founded by Charles Taze Russell in 1879 in Pennsylvania, with the current headquarters in Brooklyn, New York. Jehovah's Witnesses follow all current Watchtower publications, including the New World Translation of the Bible, Reasoning from the Scriptures, You Can Live Forever in Paradise on Earth, and the Watchtower and Awake! Magazines. They believe a person must be baptized as a Jehovah's Witness in order to be saved. Most followers must earn everlasting life on earth by "door-to-door work." Salvation in heaven is limited to 144,000

---

8. Ibid., p. 5.
9. Ibid., p. 9.

"anointed ones." This number has already been reached. The 144,000 will live as spirits in heaven. The rest of the righteous, known as "the great crowd," live on earth, where they must obey God perfectly for 1000 years or be annihilated.[10]

5. Mormonism

Mormonism was founded in 1830 by Joseph Smith, Jr. in New York. The present headquarters is in Salt Lake City. Mormons follow the Book of Mormon, Doctrine and Covenants, The Pearl of Great Price, and the King James Version of the Bible as properly interpreted by Mormon leaders. Mormons, also known as Latter-day Saints, believe they are resurrected by grace, but saved (exalted to godhood) by works, including faithfulness to church leaders, Mormon baptism, tithing, ordination, marriage, and secret temple rituals. They believe there is no eternal life without Mormon membership. Eventually, nearly everyone goes to one of three separate heavenly kingdoms, with some achieving godhood. Apostates and murderers go to "outer darkness."[11]

6. New Age

The New Age movement was popularized in part by actress Shirley MacLaine in the 1980s and 1990s. It is based on Eastern mystics, Hinduism, and paganism. New-agers have no holy book, but use selected Bible passages, I Ching, Hindu, Buddhist, Taoist writings, and Native American beliefs. They also follow writings on astrology, mysticism, and magic. They teach the need to offset bad karma with good karma. Human reincarnations occur until a

---

10. Ibid., p. 3.
11. Ibid., p. 3.

person reaches oneness with God. There is no literal heaven or hell, and there is no eternal life as a resurrected person.[12]

7. Scientology

Scientology was founded in 1954 by L. Ron Hubbard in California. Its current headquarters is in Los Angeles. Scientologists follow the book Dianetics: The Modern Science of Mental Health written by their founder. Those who follow Scientology believe there is no sin or need to repent. Salvation is freedom from reincarnation. One must work with an "auditor" on his "engrams" (hang-ups) to achieve the state of "clear," then progress up the "bridge to total freedom." To Scientologists, hell is a myth. People who get clear of engrams become operating thetans.[13]

8. Spiritualism (Spiritism)

Spiritism is an ancient belief popularized by the sisters Kate and Margaret Fox in 1848 in Hydesville, New York. This group follows various writings, including the Spiritualist Manual, Aquarian Gospel of Jesus the Christ, Oahspe, and others. Those who follow Spiritism believe a person's life continues in the spirit world after he dies. There, his spirit may progress from one level to another. Heaven and hell are just states of mind. Knowledge and good works enhance one's status in the afterlife. Some of those in the Spiritualism religion believe in reincarnation.[14]

---

12. Ibid., p. 7.
13. Ibid., p. 6.
14. Ibid., p. 6.

9. T.M. (Transcendental Meditation)

T.M. was founded in 1959 in California by Maharishi Mahesh Yogi. It is based on Hinduism and Yoga. This group follows the Hindu scriptures, including the Bhagavad-Gita, Meditations of Maharishi Mahesh Yogi, and Science of Being and the Art of Living. According to T.M., humans have forgotten their inner divinity. Salvation consists of doing good in excess of evil in order to evolve to the highest state through reincarnation. In this religion, there is no heaven or hell, only the ultimate loss of self into union with Brahman, the Hindu creator or the universe.[15]

10. Unification Church

The Unification Church was founded by Sun Myung Moon in 1954 in South Korea with its current headquarters in New York City. Moonies (followers of Mr. Moon) subscribe to the writings of their founder. These include the Divine Principle, Outline of the Principles and Level 4. They also claim to follow the Bible but claim it is not the truth itself, but a textbook teaching the truth. According to the Unification Church, salvation is achieved by obedience to and acceptance of the True Parents (Moon and his wife). This supposedly eliminates sin and results in perfection. After death, a person goes to the spirit world. There is no resurrection. Members advance by convincing others to follow Sun Myung Moon, who claims that everyone will be saved, even Satan.[16]

11. Unity (School of Christianity)

Unity was founded by Charles and Myrtle Fillmore in 1889 in

---

15. Ibid., p. 9.
16. Ibid., p. 4.

Kansas City, Missouri. Unity follows Unity magazine, Lessons in Truth, Metaphysical Bible Dictionary, and the Bible (although the Bible is not viewed as reliable as other writings). Salvation comes from believing that every person is as much a Son of God as Jesus is. There is no evil, no devil, no sin, no poverty, and no old age. A person is reincarnated until he learns these truths and becomes perfect. Death is simply the result of wrong thinking. A person moves to a different body through reincarnation until he reaches enlightenment. According to Unity, there is no heaven or hell.[17]

HOW IS CHRISTIANITY DIFFERENT?

1. Salvation is a free gift for all who believe

In reviewing the above teachings, all but one of the various religions either deny the literal existence of heaven or have a system of works by which a person can try to earn his way there. Only Biblical Christianity says heaven is a free gift to those who place their faith in Christ.

This raises several questions – Is Christianity correct? Is there a heaven, and is Jesus the only way there? Is there any real evidence to support the claims of Christianity? Is there anything that sets Christianity apart as more believable than other religions? The answer to all the questions is yes!

2. The resurrection makes Christianity unique

If God and heaven are real, it is logical that God would do something unique to show humankind the truth about Himself and the way to heaven. That is precisely what He did with Jesus. God the Father sent Christ the Son to earth to be born, to live, to die, and to

---

17. Ibid., p. 5.

conquer death. Death, perhaps more than anything else, has struck fear into the hearts of humans through the ages. It is final and mysterious. By rising from the dead on the third day after His crucifixion, Jesus proved He is what He claims to be – God in human flesh. As such, He says He is the only way to heaven. If Jesus is God, then what He says can be trusted.

Other religious leaders who teach about God and heaven have done nothing comparable to the resurrection to back up their claims. In fact, Muhammad, Buddha, Joseph Smith, Mary Baker Eddy, Charles and Myrtle Fillmore, L. Ron Hubbard, and the like are all dead. Other religious leaders still alive today, will die. None but Jesus has risen bodily from the dead.

This raises another question – is there solid evidence for an historical resurrection? Again, the answer is yes. There is more evidence for the resurrection of Jesus Christ than for any other event in ancient history. Whole books have been written about it. Although skeptics through the ages have tried to disprove the resurrection, none have been successful, and many have come to a saving knowledge of Christ in the process. The resurrection stands as undeniable truth. If you have not yet read the chapter in this book, *Is the Resurrection True?*, you are encouraged to do so. The evidence in favor of the resurrection is overwhelming.

No wonder Jesus was able to say in John 14:6, *I am the way, and the truth, and the life; no one comes to the Father, but through Me.* In this verse, He did not say He was a way to heaven – Jesus said He was *the way*. He did not say He was a truth about God; He said He was *the truth*. He did not say He was one of many options regarding life. He said He is *the life*. He didn't say that people could take many paths to God. He said no one comes to the Father but through Him!

Some people are angered by Jesus' statement about Himself. They accuse Him of arrogance or narrow-mindedness. But, if Jesus conquered death, thus proving His Deity, His statement is not arrogant or narrow-minded; it is the truth. No amount of reasoning, complaining, arguing, or denying will change it.

Consider that people need to breathe air with the right amount of oxygen in it to live. If an astronaut thought this was too restrictive and decided to remove his helmet while walking on the moon, he would die. No amount of complaining or arguing would change the fact that there are certain parameters he needs to abide by in order to remain alive. So it is with Jesus. He is the only way to eternal life with God. Listen again to His words in John 14:6, *I am the way, and the truth, and the life; no one comes to the Father but through Me.* The whole process of how a person gets to heaven will be looked at in great detail in the next chapter of this book.

So, how is Christianity different from other world religions? The answer is profound: Christians serve a risen Savior.

Other ways Christianity is different from other religions include the following:

3. God reached down to us

Most religions are just that: religions with people reaching up to God trying to earn their earn salvation or some eternal state through a series of good works. Christianity, on the other hand, says that no one can earn their way to God (Ephesians 2:8,9). Instead, God reached down to us and made a way for people to come to Him. He did it by sending Jesus (His Son) to earth to be born as a baby, to live a perfect life, and ultimately to die for us, and then to rise from the dead so that we could be forgiven and be saved by placing our trust in Him. Matthew 1:18-25 tells the story of Jesus coming to earth.

Now the birth of Jesus Christ was as follows: when His mother Mary had been betrothed to Joseph, before they came together she was found to be with child by the Holy Spirit. And Joseph her husband, being a righteous man and not wanting to disgrace her, planned to send her away secretly. But when he had considered this, behold, an angel of the Lord appeared to him in a dream, saying, "Joseph, son of David, do not be afraid to take Mary as your wife; for the Child who has been conceived in her is of the Holy Spirit. She will bear a Son; and you shall call His name Jesus, for He will save His people from their sins." Now all this took place to fulfill what was spoken by the Lord through the prophet: "BEHOLD, THE VIRGIN SHALL BE WITH CHILD AND SHALL BEAR A SON, AND THEY SHALL CALL HIS NAME IMMANUEL," which translated means, "GOD WITH US." And Joseph awoke from his sleep and did as the angel of the Lord commanded him, and took Mary as his wife, but kept her a virgin until she gave birth to a Son; and he called His name Jesus.

4. Christianity is more of a relationship rather than a religion

Christianity is not so much a religion as it is a relationship with God through Jesus. James 4:8 states, *Draw near to God and He will draw near to you.* God is not aloof from His creation but longs for people to draw near to Him. He does not force Himself on people but desires that they choose to follow and serve Him because they want to, not because they have to.

SOME OF THE BENEFITS OF BEING A CHRISTIAN

Not only is Christianity different than other religions, but the benefits of being a Christian are rather amazing. When people repent of sin and invite Jesus to come into their life, placing their faith in Him, some amazing things happen that clearly benefit them in this life and the life to come. Here are some of those benefits:

1. They receive the promise of Heaven (eternal life with God in Heaven).

John 3:16 states, *"For God so loved the world, that He gave His only begotten Son, that whoever believes in Him shall not perish, but have eternal life.* Jesus came to give eternal life to those who place their faith and trust in Him. Heaven is where people will spend eternity with God.

2. They become members of God's family.

Speaking about Jesus, John 1:12 states, *But as many as received Him, to them He gave the right to become children of God, even to those who believe in His name.* When a person believes on Jesus and places their faith in Him, that person becomes a child of God.

3. They have a new purpose – "To glorify (honor) God."

Isaiah 43:7 states, *Everyone who is called by My name, and whom I have created for My glory, whom I have formed, even whom I have made.* God created everything to bring glory (honor) to Him. Christians honor God by living lives in line with God's principles and values found in the Bible. When people live this way, their lives are a great witness to others and proof positive that they belong to Christ.

4. They receive the indwelling Holy Spirit.

When Jesus talked to His disciples about leaving them and returning to His Father in heaven, He said, *I will ask the Father, and He will give you another Helper, that He may be with you forever; that is the Spirit of truth, whom the world cannot receive, because it does not see Him or know Him, but you know Him because He abides with you and will be in you.* (John 14:16-17). The Holy Spirit would not just be with the disciples; He would be **in** them. The Bible teaches that at the moment a person places his trust in Christ, he is indwelt (Romans 8:9), baptized (1 Corinthians 12:13), and sealed (Ephesians 1:13,14) with the Holy Spirit. The Spirit is given as God's pledge that the person is saved and will go to Heaven when he dies. The indwelling Holy Spirit is the One who gives Christians strength to live the Christian life. He is also a guide who can help believers make wise decisions and avoid doing the wrong things.

5. They have a direct line to God through prayer, and He gives them inner peace.

Philippians 4:6-7 states, *Be anxious for nothing, but in everything by prayer and supplication with thanksgiving let your requests be made known to God. And the peace of God, which surpasses all comprehension, will guard your hearts and your minds in Christ Jesus.* Rather than being worried about life and its challenges, Christians can take everything to God in prayer and enjoy the inner peace that only He can give.

6. They receive God's precious promises.

The Bible is full of promises for those who place their faith in God. Each promise is quite amazing. Here are a few of God's promises to those who love and trust Him:

Deuteronomy 31:8 - *The LORD is the one who goes ahead of you; He will be with you. He will not fail you or forsake you. Do not fear or be dismayed.*

Psalm 32:8 - *I will instruct you and teach you in the way which you should go; I will counsel you with My eye upon you.*

Psalm 37:23 - *The steps of a man are established by the LORD, and He delights in his way.*

Isaiah 26:3 - *The steadfast of mind You will keep in perfect peace, because he trusts in You.*

Isaiah 41:10 – *Do not fear, for I am with you; do not anxiously look about you, for I am your God. I will strengthen you, surely I will help you, surely I will uphold you with My righteous right hand.*

Matthew 11:28-30 - *Come to Me, all who are weary and heavy-laden, and I will give you rest. Take My yoke upon you and learn from Me, for I am gentle and humble in heart, and YOU WILL FIND REST FOR YOUR SOULS. For My yoke is easy and My burden is light.*

John 16:33 - *These things I have spoken to you, so that in Me you may have peace. In the world you have tribulation, but take courage; I have overcome the world.*

Christianity, indeed, is different than any other religion! Thank God that Jesus did the one thing that no one else could ever do. He raised Himself from the dead! In John 10:18, Jesus said, *No one has taken it (My life) away from Me, but I lay it down on My own initiative. I have authority to lay it down, and I have authority to take it up again. This commandment I received from My Father.*

DISCUSSION QUESTIONS

HOW IS CHRISTIANITY DIFFERENT FROM OTHER RELIGIONS?

1. What is the main thing that sets Christianity off from other religions?

2. What other things make Christianity unique among the religions of the world?

3. Does it anger you that Jesus claims to be the only way to Heaven? Why or why not?

4. How does the astronaut illustration shared in this chapter show that the way to life is restrictive? Can you think of other examples that illustrate this same point?

5. How has this chapter affected your view of Christianity?

CHAPTER

EIGHT

HOW DOES A PERSON GET TO HEAVEN?

DO ALL ROADS LEAD TO HEAVEN?

As a new chaplain in the military, my first duty station was Nellis Air Force Base in Las Vegas, Nevada. Nine chaplains served on the staff, and the head chaplain was a Jewish rabbi. The rabbi was a gracious man and a good boss. Although we all worked in the same chapel complex, each faith group (Protestants, Catholics and Jews) had separate programs.

I'll never forget the first time the rabbi came to my office. I had just arrived and was unpacking my boxes of professional books. Everything was in disarray. As the rabbi entered, his gaze scanned the room and landed on a Jewish tract laying on the corner of my desk. Picking it up, He read the title, "Shalom" (the Hebrew word for peace). He smiled, opened the tract, and began reading silently. The tract was designed to tell Jews about Christianity. His smile turned into a bit of a frown as he looked up and said, "I'm bothered by tracts that target other religious groups." I thought this encounter would harm our relationship, but it didn't. For the next two years, as we served together, we both did our best to treat each other with respect and kindness.

On another occasion, we had an in-depth discussion on the subject of salvation. This time, it took place in the rabbi's office. He asked me if I really believed that Jesus was the only way to Heaven. I told him, "Yes." He then told me he had a different view. In his opinion, getting to Heaven was like climbing a mountain. Jews were going up one side of the mountain, Christians up another, Hindus up a third route, and so on. Even though each part of the mountain looked a bit different, one day, all the groups would meet at the top in the presence of God. At that time, they would realize they were all on the right path.

In the rabbi's view, the problem came when groups (like Christians) began traversing the mountain, trying to convince other groups they were headed the wrong way. What each group needed to do was to leave the other groups alone and simply head up the mountain. Time spent traversing was wasted time and could be spent more productively heading uphill. In addition, trying to convince other religions they were going in the wrong direction, only clouded the issue and created ill will. Everyone needed to leave everyone else alone and mind his or her own business.

Several years later, in another setting and with a different person, I heard a similar illustration. I was riding in the front seat of a hearse on the way to a funeral. As we crossed the Golden Gate Bridge, I asked the driver his opinion regarding who would be in Heaven. He responded by describing a beautiful stained-glass window. He believed the different pieces of glass – all different shapes, sizes, and colors – represented the different religious groups. Even though each group had its own beliefs, God would welcome them all into His presence.

Although both of the above illustrations are thought-provoking, are they true? Do all roads lead to God? Will God welcome all people into His presence no matter what they believe? These are two of the key questions that will be answered in this chapter.

THE GARDEN OF EDEN

You may remember the biblical account of God creating Adam and Eve. He placed them in a beautiful garden and gave them everything they needed for life and happiness. Their only prohibition was to refrain from eating fruit from the tree of the knowledge of good and evil, *And the LORD God commanded the man, saying, "From any tree of the garden you may eat freely; but from the tree of the knowledge of good and evil you shall not eat, for in the day that you eat from it you shall surely die.* (Genesis 2:16-17). Rather than heeding God's warning, Eve succumbed to Satan's temptation, ate the fruit, and gave some to Adam, who also ate. Genesis 3:1-7 records the incident,

> *Now the serpent was more crafty than any beast of the field which the LORD God had made. And he said to the woman, "Indeed, has God said, 'You shall not eat from any tree of the garden'?" And the woman said to the serpent, "From the fruit of the trees of the garden we may eat; but from the fruit of the tree which is in the middle of the garden, God has said, 'You shall not eat from it or touch it, lest you die.'" And the serpent said to the woman, "You surely shall not die! For God knows that in the day you eat from it your eyes will be opened, and you will be like God, knowing good and evil." When the woman saw that the tree was good for food, and that it was a delight to the eyes, and that the tree was desirable to make one wise, she took from its fruit and ate; and she gave also to her husband with her, and he ate. Then the eyes of both of them were opened, and they knew that they*

were naked; and they sewed fig leaves together and made themselves loin coverings.

It is interesting that after Adam and Eve sinned, they did not die physically. Did God not mean what He said, *For in the day that you eat from it you shall surely die?* Yes, He did. Actually, at the moment Adam and Eve ate from the Tree of the Knowledge of Good and Evil, they began to die physically; the aging process set in, and their days on earth were numbered. Before they ate, they could have lived indefinitely on the earth.

PHYSICAL AND SPIRITUAL DEATH

Along with the beginnings of physical death, Adam and Eve died spiritually; they became spiritually separated from God. The distinction between physical and spiritual death is important to understand. Physical death may be defined as the separation of the spirit from the body at the moment a person's bodily systems shut down. Spiritual death, on the other hand, is the separation of a person's spirit from God. It is possible for a person to be physically alive and spiritually dead. This was the case with Adam and Eve.

THE CURSE AND THE COMING MESSIAH

After Eve and Adam sinned, God pronounced a curse on them and on the serpent. This curse is found in Genesis 3:14-17. Notice especially what God says to the serpent, Satan.

And the LORD God said to the serpent, "Because you have done this, cursed are you more than all cattle, and more than every beast of the field; On your belly shall you go, and dust shall you eat all the days of your life; And I will put enmity between you and the woman, and between your seed and her seed; He shall bruise you on the head, and you shall bruise him on the heel." To the woman He said, "I will greatly multiply your pain in childbirth, in pain you shall bring forth children; yet your desire shall be for your husband, and he shall rule over you." Then to Adam He said, "Because you have listened to the voice of your wife, and have eaten from the tree about which I commanded you, saying, 'You shall not eat from it'; cursed is the ground because of you; in toil you shall eat of it all the days of your life."

Regarding Satan, God said there would be enmity (hatred) between the woman and him. God would send someone who would receive a bruised heel, but, in the process, would bruise (crush) Satan's head. This prophecy refers to the promised Messiah who would come to destroy the power of Satan even though it seemed Satan had the victory. This was fulfilled in the crucifixion and resurrection of Jesus Christ. When Jesus was crucified, it seemed Satan was victorious; but when Christ rose from the dead on the third day, it was clear He had crushed Satan's power! Having a bruised heel is not a fatal injury. Having a crushed head is!

From that first prophecy, God made it clear He intended to send a Savior who would break the curse of sin on the human race. The Old Testament prophets spoke of a coming Messiah. Jesus was the fulfillment of those prophecies.

UNDERSTANDING SIN AND ITS CONSEQUENCES

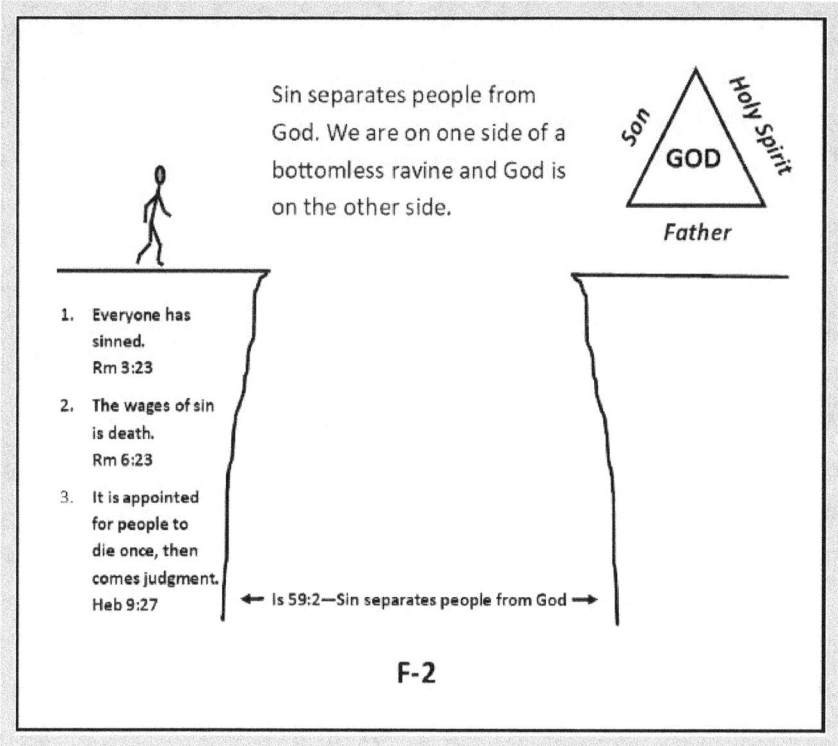

F-2

When sin entered the world through the first man and woman, the whole creation was affected. Sin separated man spiritually from God. Isaiah 59:2 states, *But your iniquities have made a separation between you and your God, and your sins have hidden His face from you, so that He does not hear.* In short, sin separates people from God. Humans are on one side of a spiritual chasm, and God is on the other. See F-2. (This is similar to the Navigator's Bridge.)

Through the seed of the man, sin passed to all subsequent generations so the Bible rightly states, *For all have sinned and fall short of the glory of God* (Romans 3:23). Simply put, every human has sinned and is under sin's curse.

To sin means to miss the mark. Picture a target. Rather than hitting the bull's-eye with our thoughts, words, and actions (the arrows of life), we often fall short of God's best. We think, say, and do things that dishonor God. Each of us has missed the mark to a greater or lesser degree. This makes us all guilty.

James 2:10 reveals, *For whoever keeps the whole law and yet stumbles in one point, he has become guilty of all.* Even one sin makes a person guilty before a holy and perfect God.

The truth is, we are not sinners because we sin; we sin because we are sinners. Every person, since the creation of Adam and Eve, has been born with a sin nature passed on from those first parents. A person's sin nature is his bent toward sin. This sin nature is clearly seen even in small children. Parents spend much of their time teaching children the right things to do because the wrong comes quite naturally.

Romans 6:23 goes on to say, *For the wages of sin is death...* Just like men are paid a wage for work, God pays a wage for sin. That wage is death, spiritual separation from Him. Each of us is under this condemnation unless we have our sin removed.

COMING JUDGMENT

Hebrews 9:27 further states, *And inasmuch as it is appointed for men to die once and after this comes judgment.* All people will die physically and then be judged. Each person has an appointment with death. God, in His omniscience (His ability to know everything – past, present and future), knows the exact day, hour, and second we will take our last breath. As long as a person is alive, he has the opportunity to have his sins forgiven. But if he dies physically before his sins are washed away, he will be eternally separated from God in Hell.

Many people have a great misconception about what happens after death. They believe everyone automatically goes either to Heaven or into a state of nothingness where there is no conscious existence. This, however, is not what the Bible teaches. Instead, Scripture clearly indicates that those who die without Christ go into an eternal, conscious existence away from God. This is a place of torment, suffering, and pain.

I have attended many funerals where people gave glowing eulogies about the deceased even though it was clear the deceased did not believe in God. The people said things like, "I know old Joe will go to Heaven because he was a wonderful husband and father," or, "I know Sally is in a better place because she did so many kind acts." As nice as these words sound, and as much as people hope they are true, they do not square with the Bible. If the Bible is God's Word, and all evidence indicates that it is, the real question is not, "What do I believe is true in regard to Heaven?" but instead, "What does the Bible teach?"

BRIDGES THAT WON'T GET A PERSON INTO HEAVEN

Mankind has tried to build many bridges to God, but none of them make it across the spiritual ravine.

First, the Bible makes it clear that doing good deeds doesn't get anyone to Heaven. There is no doubt God wants us to do good things, but Ephesians 2:8,9 makes it clear good works won't save anyone; *For by grace you have been saved through faith; and that not of yourselves, it is the gift of God; not as a result of works, that no one should boast.* If we could be saved by good works, we could boast about it; but no one will boast when they stand in front of God. Actually, as good as our good works are, they are really like filthy rags before a holy God. Isaiah 64:6 confirms this fact: *For all of us have become like one who is unclean, and all our righteous deeds are like a filthy garment;*

and all of us wither like a leaf, and our iniquities, like the wind, take us away.

Some men try to bridge the gap between man and God through religion. They go to religious meetings, pray, serve, or give to worthy causes. As good as these things are, they are religious works, and it has already been shown that works cannot save a person.

Morality is another way people try to bridge the gap. There is no doubt God wants us to live moral lives. The problem is, none of us can. We may live morally most of the time, but we will all sin sometimes. Scripture teaches that even one sin makes us guilty of God's judgment (James 2:10).

Another way men try to bridge the gap is through philosophy. They think that by embracing some belief system outside the Bible, they will be saved. What they fail to realize is that no matter how someone looks at life, he is still a sinner, and his sin separates him from God. It is easy for people today to get caught up in all sorts of belief systems that take them captive and keep them from discovering the forgiveness of sins that only comes through Christ. Colossians 2:8 says, *See to it that no one takes you captive through philosophy and empty deception, according to the tradition of men, according to the elementary principles of the world, rather than according to Christ.*

No bridge other than Christ will get a person to God. Good works, religion, morality, and philosophy all fall short. Some people aren't willing to accept this truth because they desperately want to earn their way to Heaven. The fact is, they can't!

It is interesting how many people aren't willing to accept help from others. They are perfectly willing to give help, but their own pride often keeps them from accepting help themselves. In order to come to God, a person has to put his pride aside and admit he is powerless to earn his own way to Heaven. For some people who have a lot of money, possessions or worldly success, this is a hard pill to swallow. They have been used to solving their own problems and making their own way in life. They have a hard time accepting the fact they can't earn salvation. Their hard work may get them great rewards in this life, but it will not get them into the next. If people want to spend eternity with God, they have to humble themselves and admit they need God's help.

F-3 shows a summary of the plan of salvation to this point.

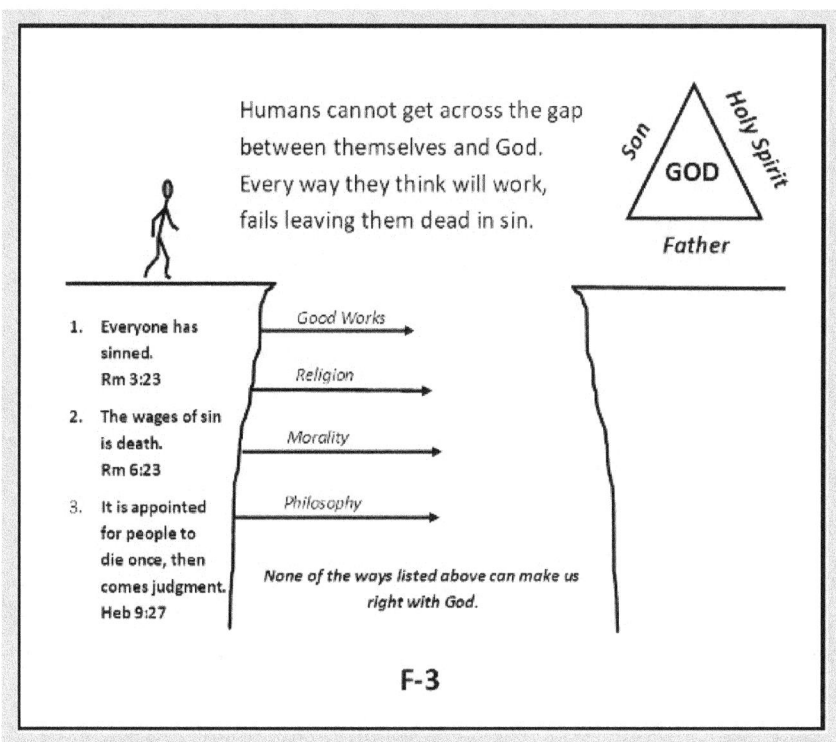

F-3

JESUS IS THE ONLY WAY TO HEAVEN

Romans 5:8,9 states, *But God demonstrates His own love toward us, in that while we were yet sinners, Christ died for us. Much more then, having now been justified by His blood, we shall be saved from the wrath of God through Him.*

While we were spiritually dead in sin, God made a way for us to get to Him. That way is Jesus Christ. Jesus came to die for our sin in order that He might bring us to God. 1 Peter 3:18 states, *For Christ also died for sins once for all, the just for the unjust, in order that He might bring us to God, having been put to death in the flesh, but made alive in the spirit.*

Even though Jesus died in order to bring us to God, salvation is not automatic. It comes through faith.

HEAD AND HEART BELIEF

John 3:16-18 states,

> *For God so loved the world, that He gave His only begotten Son, that whoever believes in Him should not perish, but have eternal life. For God did not send the Son into the world to judge the world, but that the world should be saved through Him. He who believes in Him is not judged; he who does not believe has been judged already, because he has not believed in the name of the only begotten Son of God.*

In order to be saved, a person must believe in Christ. If all a person has to do is believe, it is critical to understand what the word *believe* means. In John 3:16 *believe* means two things. First it means head-belief, believing something intellectually. Second, it means heart-belief, being wholeheartedly committed to it. The difference between these two can be understood through the illustration of a footbridge spanning a deep canyon. A person could say, "I believe the bridge will hold me." This is head-belief. To really believe in the bridge, he must actually walk across it.

Only then has he exercised wholehearted commitment (heart-belief).

Putting one's faith in Christ is more than having head-belief. James 2:19 states, *You believe that God is one. You do well; the demons also believe, and shudder.* The demons have head-belief about God, but they do not follow Him, and in the end, they will be doomed to Hell. There's a big difference between believing something about God and believing in God. It is only when a person commits to follow Christ wholeheartedly that he truly believes. The good thing is, unlike a footbridge, Jesus will never fail.

RECEIVING JESUS AS LORD AND SAVIOR

But how does a person make this commitment to follow Jesus? John 1:12 states that it is done by receiving Christ, *But as many as received Him, to them He gave the right to become children of God, even to those who believe in His name.* Receiving equals believing. How does a person receive Christ? Romans 10:9-11 states that he does it through prayer.

> *If you confess with your mouth Jesus as Lord, and believe in your heart that God raised Him from the dead, you shall be saved; for with the heart man believes, resulting in righteousness, and with the mouth he confesses, resulting in salvation. For the Scripture says, "Whoever believes in Him will not be disappointed."*

Notice what comes out of the mouth must also be in the heart. A person confesses with his mouth but believes in his heart. Notice, too, a person must confess Jesus as Lord. This means to invite Christ to take control of one's life by giving Him the freedom to call the shots. Many people want Jesus to save them but do not want Him to be in charge. They want to know they are going to Heaven, but they do not want Jesus meddling with their bad habits, wrong attitudes, or sinful behavior. But Jesus doesn't just come as Savior; He comes as Lord and Savior! Think of it this way: if a person wants Jesus as Savior, he may or may not want Him as Lord. But if the same person asks Jesus to be his Lord, he obviously wants Him as Savior. Someone rightly said, "When a person asks Christ to save him, he must also invite Jesus to be his Lord. He must turn over the reins of control of his life to the Master, even though he may not understand all of the ramifications. He willingly needs to say, "Jesus, here I am, forgive my sin, and be my Lord. Take control of my life and make me what you want me to be." If a person does this whole-heartedly, he will be saved! F-4 shows how Jesus bridges the gap between God and man.

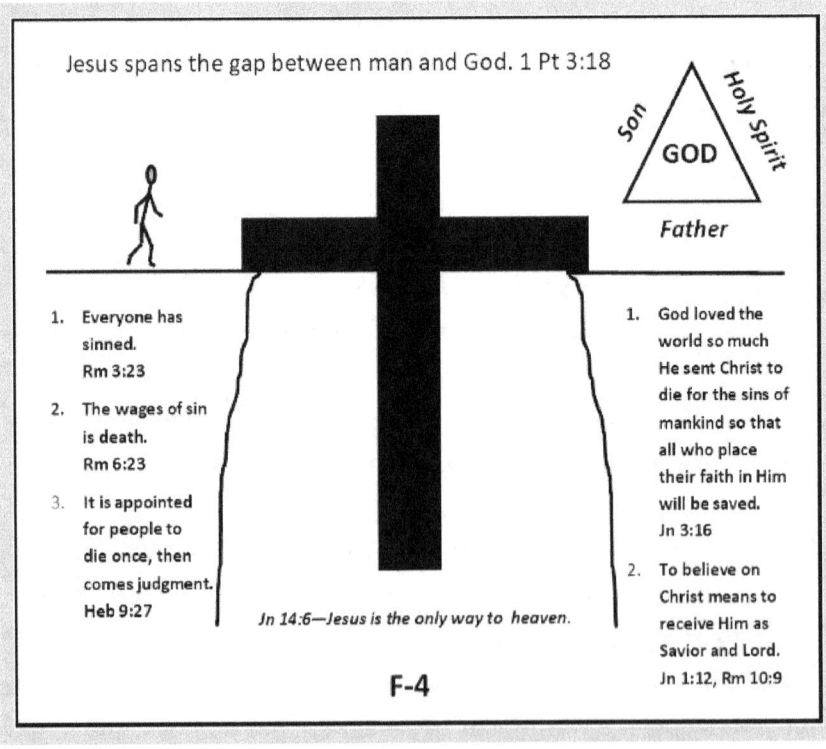

Jesus spans the gap between man and God. 1 Pt 3:18

Son / Holy Spirit / GOD / Father

1. Everyone has sinned. Rm 3:23
2. The wages of sin is death. Rm 6:23
3. It is appointed for people to die once, then comes judgment. Heb 9:27

Jn 14:6—Jesus is the only way to heaven.

1. God loved the world so much He sent Christ to die for the sins of mankind so that all who place their faith in Him will be saved. Jn 3:16
2. To believe on Christ means to receive Him as Savior and Lord. Jn 1:12, Rm 10:9

F-4

The following is a simple prayer a person can use to ask Christ into his heart to be Lord and Savior. If you have never responded to Christ in this way, you are encouraged to pray the following prayer from the depth of your heart.

Dear Jesus. I need you. I admit that I am a sinner and that my sin separates me from You. Thank You for dying for my sin on the cross and for rising on the third day to prove You are God. Thank You for making a way for me to go to Heaven. I ask You to come into my life through the power of the Holy Spirit, to forgive my sin, and to make me the person You want me to be. I give myself wholeheartedly to You. Be my Lord and Savior. AMEN

If you prayed this prayer and meant it, congratulations! You are now a child of God. Your salvation is not based on your own merit, but on Christ's sacrificial death for you.

When you die and stand before God, if He asks you, "Why should you be allowed to enter My Heaven?", you can say, "I should be allowed in because I received Jesus as Lord and Savior. It is His sacrifice that washes away my sin." God will then say something like, "Enter My child into the joy of your salvation."

THE ASSURANCE OF SALVATION

Another bit of great news is that once a person is truly saved (He sincerely invites Christ into his life to be Lord and Savior), he cannot lose his salvation.

1 John 5:11-13 states,

And the witness is this, that God has given us eternal life, and this life is in His Son. He who has the Son has the life; he who does not

have the Son of God does not have the life. These things I have written to you who believe in the name of the Son of God, in order that you may know that you have eternal life.

Just as a child who is born into a family cannot be unborn, so, too, a person born into God's family cannot be unborn. He is a child of God, and his salvation is secure! That is not to say he won't sin. He will, and he will need to ask forgiveness when he does, but he won't lose his salvation.

God's desire for every one of His children is for them to live for Him each day, to grow in their faith, and to be good representatives for the kingdom of God.

The Christian life is not an easy life. In fact, it is an impossible life without the indwelling power of the Holy Spirit. But, it is the best life. There will be struggles and challenges, but there will also be great joy and blessing.

If a person hopes to live the Christian life, it will be helpful to study the Bible each day, pray, worship weekly in a good church, and find other Christians (perhaps become part of a small group in his local church) where he can fellowship and be held accountable. He will also need to find a place of service and be willing to share his faith with non-Christians when God gives the opportunity. Doing these things does not earn a person salvation, but will prove to be helpful in the process of growing in faith.

FINAL THOUGHTS

Jesus is Lord. As Lord, He invites people to respond to Him by asking Him to be their personal Lord and Savior. If you have responded to Christ in this way, praise God! May you walk with Him each day and may you share His good news with others so they, too, will find salvation.

If you are a follower of Jesus, you are His **disciple**, which means **a learner**, one who learns more about his faith so he can apply it to life and please the Lord in the things he thinks, says and does. Examples are:

- Learning to love unconditionally,
- Learning to forgive like Jesus, and
- Putting the needs of others before your own.

As you learn and apply God's truth, you will be equipped to lead others to Christ and to help them grow in their faith. We were made disciples in order to make disciples. This is Christ's Great Commission to His followers. Matthew 28:18-20 states.

*And Jesus came up and spoke to them, saying, "All authority has been given to Me in heaven and on earth. **Go** therefore and **make disciples** of all the nations, **baptizing** them in the name of the Father and the Son and the Holy Spirit, **teaching** them to observe all that I commanded you; and lo, I am with you always, even to the end of the age."*

It is every believer's privilege to be part of living for God and helping others live for Him, too. Have a very blessed life!

DISCUSSION QUESTIONS

HOW DOES A PERSON GET TO HEAVEN?

1. How has the information in this book affected your view regarding the way a person gets to Heaven?

2. What are some views you have heard regarding how people get to Heaven?

3. How does the resurrection of Jesus set Christianity apart from other religions?

4. Assuming Christianity is true, why, in your opinion, would God make Jesus the only way to Heaven? Is there anything in the world around us that indicates the path to life is sometimes narrow?

5. What are the five major world religions, and what do they teach about salvation?

6. Take a few moments to study Figure 3 (F-3) in this booklet, and then try to explain it in your own words.

7. Have you asked Jesus Christ to come into your life to be your personal Lord and Savior? If so, when did it happen, and what were the circumstances surrounding your decision?

8. If you have not received Christ into your life, what is holding you back?

9. What questions do you still need answered before you would be willing to make the decision to become a Christian?

ACKNOWLEDGMENTS

I am grateful to Frank Eastland and his staff at Publish Authority for their expertise, encouragement, and support during every phase of the publishing process. At Publish Authority, I am most grateful to Janet Silburn for her thorough and excellent editing work, and kudos also to Raeghan Rebstock for designing a fabulous book cover. In addition, thanks to my wife, Sharon, for her constant encouragement during the writing phase and to our friends Mary Enbom and Sibylla Ortiz for their early editing. Without the help of everyone mentioned, this book would never have made it into the hands of readers. I am eternally grateful to God for each one of you.

Finally, special thanks to all who purchase the "Christian Answers Course" for reading themselves and/or giving it to a friend to read. It is my hope that this book influences people to come to a saving knowledge of Jesus Christ and grow in their walk with Him.

ABOUT THE AUTHOR

Chris Losey grew up in Calistoga, California, in the beautiful Napa Valley. He received his Bachelor of Science degree from the United States Military Academy at West Point, New York, in 1973. After serving for five years as an infantry officer in the Army, he resigned his commission and returned to school, receiving his Master of Divinity degree from Western Conservative Baptist Seminary in Portland, Oregon, in 1982. During that time, he also served in the Army Reserve. After graduating from Western, Chris returned to active-duty military service, where he served as an Air Force Chaplain, retiring in 1994. For the next twenty years, he served as senior pastor of Valley Baptist Church in San Rafael, California, retiring a second time in 2014 due to Parkinson's disease. In 2017, Chris had successful Deep Brain Stimulation surgery for Parkinson's and is now an advocate for the procedure.

Chris and his wife Sharon have been married for 50 years and enjoy life in Elk Grove, California, where they serve as volunteers in their local church. They have two children and eight grandchildren. Chris and Sharon enjoy walking, golfing, and living close to family. Chris also enjoys writing music and singing.

To learn more about the author, visit his website, "Building Godly Families." It offers a variety of free resources at ChrisLosey.com.

REFERENCES

Chapter 2 – Is the Bible God's Word?

Evans, William , *Great Doctrines of the Bible,* Bibliotech Press, 2019

Norman L. Geisler and William E. Nix, *A General Introduction to the Bible*, Moody Press, 1968.

Morris, Henry M, *The Bible and Modern Science,* Moody Press, 1968.

Chapter 3 – Who is Jesus

Josephus, *Antiquities of the Jews,* John C. Winston Company, (no publication date).

Chapter 6 – Has Science Disproved the Bible? Is Evolution True?

Morris, Henry M, *The Bible and Modern Science*, Moody Press, 1968.

S. I. McMillen,, S.L, Stern, *None of These Diseases*, Fleming H. Revell Company, 1984.

Blick, Edward F, *Correlation of the Bible & Science*, Southwest Radio Church, 1988.

Geisler, Norman L, *Baker Encyclopedia of Christian Apologetics*, Baker Books, 1999

Morris, Henry M, *Scientific Creationism*, Mater Books, 1985

Johnson, Phillip E, *Darwin on Trial*, Intervarsity Press, 1993.

World Book Multimedia Encyclopedia, 1991

Darwin, Charles, On the Origin of Species, Barnes and Noble Classics, 2008.

Gould, Stephen Jay, "Evolution's Erratic Pace." *Natural History*, 86, 5; 12-17, May 1977. https://eric.ed.gov/?id=EJ160937.

Morris, Henry M, *Evolution and the Modern Christian*, Baker Book House, 1967.

Chapter 7 – How is Christianity Different from Other Religions?

Christianity, Cults and Religions, Rose Publishing, 2000.

Ridenour, Fritz, *So What's the Difference?* Regal Books, 1970.

OTHER HELPFUL BOOKS

Case for Christ, Lee Strobel, Zondervan Publishing, 1998

Case for A Creator, Lee Strobel, Zondervan Publishing, 2014

Case for Faith, Lee Strobel, Zondervan Publishing, 2021

Debunking Evolution, Daniel Biddle, Genesis Apologetics, 2016. A six-lesson video-based training program for Christian students from junior high school to college.

Evolution: A Theory in Crisis, Michael Denton, Aldar and Aldar Publishing, 1986
The book gathers evidence against evolution. It is a clear account of a growing crisis in biology and helps us understand why an increasing number of research scientists are questioning the validity of the theory of evolution.

Evolution: The Challenge of the Fossil Record, Duane Gish, Creation Life Publishers, 1985
This book contains all the information needed to challenge the theory of evolution regarding the fossil record. It is put in easy-to-understand language with great illustrations.

From Goo to You by Way of the Zoo, Harold Hill, Fleming and Revell, 1985
This entertaining book totally debunks the theory of evolution by taking a close look at Radiometric Dating and the fossil record. It shows clearly how many people have been duped into believing a theory through evidence which is obvious to the casual observer if he will simply get himself informed.

Scientific Creationism, Henry M. Morris, Ph.D., Master Books, 1985
This book is a must-read regarding information on the bankrupt theory of macro-evolution. It is the quintessential volume that shows why special creation is true and evolution is false.

For a more in-depth study of the reasons why the resurrection is true, I highly recommend these best-selling books: *Evidence that Demands A Verdict* and *More Evidence that Demands A Verdict* by Josh McDowell (Thomas Nelson Publishing,

2017; Campus Crusade for Christ, 1975). It is interesting to note that McDowell was one of those skeptics who set out to disprove the resurrection and became a Christian in the process.

Kingdom of the Cults, Walter Martin, Walter Martin Publishing, 1977.